Southern Living

Entryways

Oxmoor
House®

Southern Living® Entryways was adapted from a book by the same title published by Sunset Books.

Consulting Editors: Richard Day, Timothy Thoelecke, Don Vandervort, Jane Horn
Editorial Coordinators: Bradford Kachelhofer, Vicki Weathers
Senior Editor: Jim McRae
Editor: Rob Lutes
Art Director: Jean-Pierre Bourgeois
Writers: Stacey Berman, Ned Meredith
Picture Editor: Jennifer Meltzer
Special Contributors: Lisa Anderson, La Bande Créative, Gilles Beauchemin, Bridget Bradley, Linda Cardella Cournoyer, Jean-Guy Doiron, Lorraine Doré, Martin Francoeur, Dominique Gagné, Sara Grynspan, Robert Labelle, Joan McKenna, Jennifer Ormston, Tishana Peebles, Jacques Perrault, Edward Renaud, Jean Sirois, Jean Warboy, Judy Yelon

Our appreciation to the staff of *Southern Living* magazine for their contributions to this book.

Cover:
Design: James Boone, Vasken Guiragossian
Photography: Van Chaplin, Southern Progress Photo Collection

First printing January 2000
Copyright © 2000 by Oxmoor House, Inc.
Book Division of Southern Progress Corporation
P.O. Box 2463
Birmingham, Alabama 35201
All rights reserved, including the right of reproduction in whole or in part in any form.

Southern Living® is a federally registered trademark of Southern Living, Inc.

ISBN: 0-376-09070-7
Library of Congress Catalog Card Number: 99-65010
Printed in the United States

Thanks to the Following:
Americans With Disabilities Act Service Center (ADA), Salem, MA; APA-The Engineered Wood Association, Tacoma, WA; Jon Arno, Troy, MI; Baldwin Hardware Corporation, Reading, PA; Bruce Burch, Burch, Burch, and Burch, AIA, Ltd., Wheeling, IL; Sammy Dalva, Sico Canada, Inc., Outremont, Que.; Emco Enterprises, Inc. Des Moines, Iowa; Glen-Gery Corporation, Wyomissing, PA; Cara Hancox, Hudson, Que.; Holmes Garage Door Co., Auburn, WA; HomeStyles Publishing and Marketing Inc., St. Paul, MN; Honeywell, Inc., Minneapolis, MN; Tom Hughes, Lynchburg, VA; Kestrel Shutters, Saint Peters Village, PA; Marvin Windows & Doors Warroad, MN; MKM Communications, Schaumberg, IL; National Association of Home Builders, Upper Marlboro, MD; Presso-Matic Keyless Locks, Sanford, FL; Sears, Roebuck and Co. Hoffman Estates, IL

CONTENTS

APPEALING ENTRANCES

To paraphrase an old adage, you never get a second chance to make a good first impression. This is just as true when showing off your house as it is when meeting someone for the first time. Certain houses are undeniably attractive at first glance. They have genuine "curb appeal," something that sets them apart from more run-of-the-mill houses. Every good-looking house has particular strengths that create its allure. In the photos on the following pages, you'll see houses in a variety of styles, each boasting certain elements or features that play a big part in its visual appeal. These features range from imaginative landscaping to architectural additions; from striking color schemes to flowering window boxes. As you look through the photos you'll get a better idea of just what constitutes curb appeal, and with the information presented in the rest of the book, you'll find ideas you can use to ensure your house will always make a good first impression.

The broad limestone terrace of this San Antonio home provides a graceful approach to the front door, built from salvaged barn wood. Three pairs of handsome French doors that run the length of the terrace add a pleasant symmetry.

The charm of this house is accentuated by traditional features such as shutters, window boxes, and wood siding. The carefully tended shrubs add eye-catching shapes and textures to the landscape.

A lush multilevel flower garden, complete with sparkling water feature, turns a hilly front lawn (right) into an entryway asset. For more on landscaping, see page 84.

A raised flower bed (left), encircled by stones that match the facade of the house, creates a striking front yard focal point.

Instead of a plain walk, a small entry court directs guests around the corner to the front door. The paving has the look of a terrace, thanks to tile insets that match the roof color.

1395

LA CASITA

The distinctive stone facade and flagstone driveway give this house a look of timelessness, while the yellow trim and red flowers provide lively accents.

From the stacked stone walls and flower beds at street side to the brick walkways that curve around the front lawn, this charming cottage says "welcome."

Paved with brick and mortar and outlined by a pair of short, formal hedges, a gently curving path leads graciously to the front door (below). The design is not only visually interesting, but gives the trees on the right plenty of room to grow without getting in the way. Front paths are discussed on page 68.

's hard to believe that this Lousiana raised cottage was once a dated split level house. The remodeled result,
ith entry on the main level or second floor, now looks right at home alongside the quaint cottages and
aditional Colonial-style homes on neighboring streets.

A balustrade along the edge of the roof and an impressive entry porch give the single story house above added dimension and interest.

Four colors of pavers were mixed in this entry walk: Charcoal gray, tan, and gray-and-tan mixed pavers predominate, while a smattering of red-and-charcoal pavers were included as accents.

Small touches can make a big difference. Architectural details, such as columns, a railing, and a solid fanlight enhance the front door. Thoughtful landscaping provides an inviting, informal entry garden.

Designed with severe angles, this Florida house is entered via a private court in its center that funnels breezes throughout the rooms when all of the doors are open.

An impressive entry court reinforces the similarities between this formal home and the French country estates that inspired it.

cored stucco gives the effect of rusticated stonework at the entry to
his Florida house, and breaks down its massive look. The stucco also
elps to insulate the house, an nice bonus in a tropical climate.

Textured brick, decorative half timbers, hand-carved bargeboards along the gable ends, and an old-fashioned lantern add character to the exterior of this Florida house.

...ld color and a casual front-yard garden ...ake this house memorable (facing page).

A portico clearly defines this home's entry. Substantial columns and a simple, tailored handrail give both structural and visual support.

A bright red roof, an eyebrow pediment supported by oversize brackets at the front door, and three shed dormers create an engaging facade.

A subtle lighting scheme shows off various elements of the unique entryway above. Rows of tiny lights on the steps are both an interesting design element and a safety feature. For more about lighting, see page 94.

Not a traditional foyer, but a front gallery, enriched by a Pennsylvania bluestone floor, stone walls, and exposed beams, runs the length of the main living areas. For more about foyers, see page 78.

Semicircles of stone (right) make a simple but attractive front step design in keeping with the facade of this house. Delicate flowers contrast with the weightiness of the stone.

This low stone wall, designed for sitting, encloses one side of an entry terrace.

A white picket fence sets off a charming old farmhouse (below) and provides a backdrop for colorful flowers. For more on fences, see page 104.

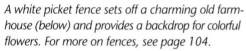

ve-green shutters and gray patterned
ling (above) create a subtle color
heme that leaves a strong impression.

Formal wrought-iron gates and a retaining wall enclose a cut-stone driveway set well away from the house. Container plants add accent colors.

Originally the front steps of this house were hidden on one side of the porch. A new stone landing, framed by dry stacked wall, forms a welcoming entrance and a clear route to the front door.

White classical columns and trim set off the distinctive shingled facade of the house above. Discreet plantings in curved beds outline the perimeter of the house.

Once this charming bungalow had all the appeal of a slice of white bread, except to the new owner who saw its potential. Now it's a little gem, thanks to added corner columns, updated paint scheme, a leaded-glass front door, and well-planned landscaping.

PLANNING YOUR ENTRYWAY

Creating a warm, inviting, and integrated entryway for your home requires careful planning. For your efforts to be successful, every alteration or addition you make, either to the house or the landscape, must work within the larger curbside view of the home.

The range of design decisions you will need to make is vast. Everything from the landscape that lies before the house to the siding and other architectural features that cover its face will come into play. The following chapter will provide you with information to help you conceive changes for your entryway and then get the job done successfully.

Entryway Basics defines the scope of entryways and offers some suggestions for when it comes time to make changes. A section on designing *(page 24)* will enlighten you on the most important dos and don'ts at this critical stage. Pages 26 and 27 focus on how to work successfully with professionals. Finally, the chapter features three before and after illustrations rendered by a designer, demonstrating the wide range of possibilities open to you as you plan your entryway.

This front yard provides everything the owners wanted—off-street parking, privacy plantings, a terrace for sitting or greeting guests, and a carefree perennial bed. Successful entryway design depends on landscape and architecture working hand in hand.

ENTRYWAY BASICS

Your home's entryway—its front facade and the landscape surrounding it—creates people's first impressions of your home. This is why the entryway is so often revamped by homeowners.

The landscape is a popular area for changes because they can usually be made more easily than changes to the house. Except in the most unusual circumstances, however, the focal point of the entryway will be the house's front. This means thinking about everything from the siding and roofing to smaller details like windows, doors, and trim when considering improvements.

As you begin planning your entryway, take time to consider what type of emotional response you want it to elicit. Elements alone and in various combinations evoke various responses. For example, bright colors convey a feeling of excitement, sunlight an atmosphere of friendliness. Emphasized proportion or height gives the impression of status, whereas symmetry of design causes a feeling of tranquillity. Your goal is to select the elements that achieve the response you want. Sketches, even crude in nature, will help you visualize different arrangements and anticipate your reaction to them.

This book contains dozens of ideas for improving your entryway. For more ideas, look through homeowner magazines and tour your neighborhood. Don't be afraid to try something a little out of the ordinary. As long as the changes you propose are successfully realized, your renewed entryway will only add to the diversity and attractiveness of the neighborhood where you live.

Potted plants and a classic bench bring style to this delightful entryway. Brass accents—the kickplate and door knocker—plus a lantern-style porch light, convey a feeling of country elegance.

ELEMENTS OF DESIGN

A well-designed entryway is an irresistible lure; you are struck by it from the street; you stroll into it and are immediately drawn to the front door. It is inviting, warm, and evokes the emotional response you want. It not only provides all the functional amenities you require, it blends them in an appealing manner. The following general design principles will help you achieve such an entryway for your home. Before making major changes to the landscape or the front of your home, however, it is best to consult with a qualified design professional.

Order: For both the front yard and the front facade of your home, the design should provide a framework or structure to the physical space. It should have a logic to it. Visual order also plays a key role; the views and lines should work together. The front of the home will already incorporate many different types of lines—vertical, horizontal, diagonal, curved, and angular—but often, one predominates and characterizes the design. Vertical lines lend a sense of height, and grandeur; horizontal lines add width and a feeling of stability; diagonals suggest movement; curved and angular lines

impart a feeling of grace and dynamism. In the landscape, the views, lines, property configuration, and circulation patterns must work together.

Dominance: To create dominance in a landscape, you can introduce focal points or specimens—an interesting tree or a sculpture. Focal points can be used to create links between different activity areas, and to lead the eye from one feature to another, creating a feeling of movement. More than one dominant feature is possible, but each should dominate a different space or view. On the home front, dominance is created by using decorative features as focal points, or by emphasizing or subduing certain lines in particular areas of the facade.

Unity: In a unified entryway, all the elements work together. Strong, observable lines and the repetition of geometric shapes contribute to a sense of unity, as does simplicity—for example, using just a few harmonizing colors in the structural elements and plantings. This does not mean that the same shape or color should be repeated throughout an entryway—carried too far, that becomes monotonous. Instead, even when the shapes of various elements

This home illustrates several of the design elements discussed in ths section. Order and unity are demonstrated by the repetition of strong angular roof lines and arches over the garage door and some of the windows. Unity is further heightened by the use of simple colors: mottled brick in shades of sandstone, pink, and gray is complemented by cedar shingles and wood trim, plus copper roofs over the portico and front bay.

The color wheel (right) illustrates the relationship between primary, secondary, and tertiary colors. Mixing adjacent primary colors on the wheel—red, yellow, and blue—creates the secondary colors—orange, green, and violet. Adjacent primary and secondary colors can then be mixed to create the tertiary colors.

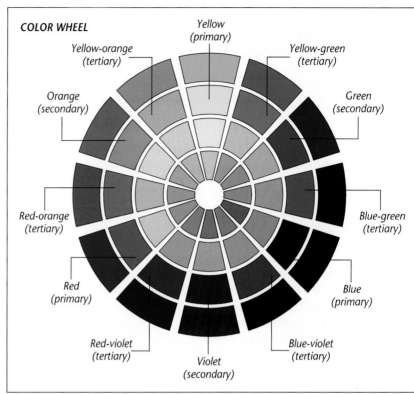

COLOR WHEEL

Yellow (primary)

Yellow-orange (tertiary)

Yellow-green (tertiary)

Orange (secondary)

Green (secondary)

Red-orange (tertiary)

Blue-green (tertiary)

Red (primary)

Blue (primary)

Red-violet (tertiary)

Blue-violet (tertiary)

Violet (secondary)

are different, their shapes can be similar or their arrangement balanced for an overall effect. Consider the shapes created by doorways, windows, shutters, and other elements. Consider new ways to complement existing shapes or add compatible new ones.

Balance: The design doesn't need to be symmetrical, but the elements should provide the same visual weight on either side of a center of interest. For example, in a front yard, you can balance a mature tree on one side of your door with perimeter benches on the other.

Proportion: In a well-designed entryway, the various elements are in proportion with one another. Your house will largely determine proportion in your landscape. All architectural elements should blend together in the facade of your home. Smaller items arranged in a group help balance a larger item, making it seem less obtrusive. Size is not the only factor here. The color, light intensity, and positioning of the elements relative to the viewer also will affect proportion. When planning for trees or other landscape elements, keep their ultimate sizes and shapes in mind. Though a tree when young may suit your front yard, it could overwhelm your house as it matures. If you find it hard to imagine a sapling's final size and shape, look at mature specimens.

Variety: In planning your entryway, try to break up monotonous areas of your landscape or home facade. Select plants in a variety of shapes, shades, and textures; or add interest by juxtaposing different materials. Imagine the pleasant surprise afforded by spotting a copper beech among greenery, a sculpture around a bend in a path, or a break in a screening hedge that reveals a view of distant hills. In the same way, consider using decorations and adding architectural details to the home facade that, while blending with the rest of the home, still create some diversion for the eye and add character to the entire entryway. Shutters, moldings, siding patterns, railings and balusters, and post lights are just a few examples.

Color: The most intimidating element of design is also the most exciting—color. As you ponder changing the color of your home or adding colors to the landscape, consider your preferences and the part of the home or landscape you're changing. Though you may love a certain bold, bright color, seeing it daily may be another matter. Keep in mind that the home is the most prominent feature in the landscape; its color or colors should harmonize with those of the other landscape elements in your entryway.

In order to determine the most effective way to use color, you'll first need to understand the color wheel *(above)*. From the primary colors of red, yellow, and blue, come all the other colors.

Skillful use of color weaves magic throughout an entryway, affecting how you perceive the home and how you feel when looking at it. Rich, warm colors make a home seem more intimate. Oranges, yellows, or colors with a red tone impart a feeling of warmth; blues, greens, or colors with a violet tone make an area seem cool. Properly applied, color can accentuate or camouflage architectural features. If you want to highlight a special area, combine bold splashes of color and light. Subtle colors can be used to hide awkward details. Many other variables, such as surfaces, textures, and surrounding colors, can also affect color. For example, a hue appears glossy on a hard smooth surface; yet on a more absorbent surface, the same color looks duller. As you narrow down your selections, make a sample board to see how your choices work together. For example, when planting flowers, you should, in general, stick to harmonious colors representing a continuous segment of the color wheel: red, red violet, and violet, for example. Use complementary colors—those opposite on the color wheel—sparingly, for accents.

GETTING THE WORK DONE

The effort you can contribute to any renovation of your home's entryway depends on your knowledge, your abilities, your patience, and your physical strength. Some jobs you can do yourself; for others, you may require professional help. For example, you may prefer to do only the nonspecialized work, such as preparing the site and cleaning up afterwards, but hire experts to do everything else. Or you may decide to do all the work yourself. Regardless of how you plan to tackle the job, consider consulting with landscape and building architects during the planning stages of the job. These professionals can help you set objectives, analyze the site, and produce detailed working plans. Some will also send out bids, help you select a contractor, specify materials for the contractor to order, and supervise the contractor's performance to ensure that your plans and time schedule are being followed. A professional will be able to advise you on local building codes that may govern some of the changes you plan to make. He or she will also assume responsibility for locating any possible problems, such as underground utilities that must be avoided as excavation is carried out. Some landscape architects have crews that work under their supervision to carry out the work they have planned. You can also consult with a landscape designer, who will often have a landscape architect's education and training, but not a state license. These professionals can generally offer the same services as a landscape architect, and are sometimes more experienced in residential projects.

If you hire people to do the work for you, building and landscape contractors will likely be the ones to do it. Building contractors are trained in construction.

A new wooden walkway expands to an intimate patio on the far side complemented by lush plantings. Creating an integrated entryway requires a developed sense of design, landscaping experience, and some carpentry skills. If you choose to contract the work to professionals, be sure to assemble everyone during the planning process so they can consult on the design and the work schedule.

A successful landscape design is often the product of landscape contractors and designers who are trained in the design and implementation of attractive and functional accents to landscaping. These professionals can handle plantings and irrigation systems, and also help ensure that the additions mesh well with the style of your property.

Landscape contractors are trained to install landscapes: plantings, pavings, structures, and irrigation systems. Either may also offer design services. On a large project, the contractor assumes the responsibility for hiring and supervising the subcontractors, if any are required.

At both the design and work stages, finding a competent person to make changes to your entryway is not always a simple task. The following are some suggestions for finding the right professional for the job and making sure the desired work gets done to your complete satisfaction.

* Ask friends and neighbors to recommend someone who's done work for them. There's nothing like a personal recommendation from someone whose judgment you trust.

* Ask the professional for references from former clients. Call these people to ask about their level of satisfaction with the work—such as whether the job was done on time, and whether it was completed within the estimated budget.

* Choose someone who's a member of a professional association. Membership does not guarantee quality, but it does indicate a willingness to conform to the rules and regulations of the organization, and to submit to peer review. Contact the American Institute of Architects (AIA), the American Society of Landscape Architects (ASLA), or the Association of Professional Landscape Designers (APLD) for referrals to professionals in your area.

* In order to compare work, and quotes, always interview more than one professional.

* Don't make your selection based on money alone; look for a reasonable cost that you can afford, coupled with good credentials and references.

* Always draw up a contract. Include the names and signatures of both you and the professional, the address where the work is to be done, specific descriptions of the materials and work involved, and the agreed time schedule and payment plan. A contract protects both you and the professional, and minimizes the chances of misunderstandings later.

ENTRYWAY MAKEOVER: TWO-STORY SUBURBAN

I t is common in modern suburban homes for the garage door to dominate the entryway. In situations such as these, creative landscaping and architecture can highlight the front door and help lead visitors there.

In the before/after example at right, a narrow concrete walkway is replaced with a wider, more inviting walk. Balanced plantings—ground covers, perennials, colorful annuals, shrubs and a mid-sized flowering tree—add beauty and direct attention toward the entry of the home.

In these cases, when the front door is less conspicuous, it also helps to make the architecture immediately surrounding it more inviting. Here decorative columns replace iron posts, while curved molding has been added along the eaves to further identify it as the primary place of entry. As a final touch, a wide skylight is installed in the roof above the door, transforming what was a relatively dark entry area into a bright, welcoming one, bathed in natural light.

The most prominent (and most problematic) feature of the entryway, the garage, is fitted with a replacement panel door, dentil molding to match the house, and lattice on one wall. Altogether, the makeover transforms a once bland entryway into a well-coordinated design and a striking curbside view.

ENTRYWAY DESIGN: TIMOTHY THOELECKE JR., APLD, ASLA, GARDEN CONCEPTS, INC. & BRUCE BURCH, BURCH, BURCH, & BURCH, AIA, LTD.

Before/After

The front of this home is transformed by several changes. Dentil molding adds traditional charm as do the larger shutters with panels below the windows replacing the louver-style shutters of the original design. Large corner columns help to direct attention to the entry area, while a large skylight gives the area a friendly air. Also to this end, the window above the entry is relocated so that it is centered over the skylight. Curved molding and large wooden columns add character. A panel door is installed to improve the garage front, while lattice covers its most conspicuous wall. In the yard, a wider pathway invites guests to the home and copious plantings add color.

ENTRYWAY MAKEOVER: RANCH HOUSE

This comely ranch-style home benefits enormously from a face-lift to its entryway. What is a relatively plain but attractive exterior becomes both more interesting and more inviting with the addition of generous plantings, a fence, walkway, and selected architectural improvements.

Because the house design is already attractive, no major work is required to create a striking entryway. In fact, the one serious problem is that the entry itself is poorly defined—a problem that is neatly solved by adding a gable over the doorway, and fencing leading up to the door. The circular windows on the gables on the right of the house are balanced with the addition of a circular window above the garage.

The relatively large front yard allows for extensive landscape work. The fence, pathways, and plantings—ground covers, annuals, perennials, and small shrubs—extending to the driveway and into the lawn, act like outstretched hands, welcoming visitors even before they get near the house. The plantings add color and variety while the diagonal lines of the beds, walkway, and railing impart a feeling of movement to the entryway as a whole.

ARCHITECT: JEROLD AXELROD & ASSOCIATES
BLUEPRINT PROVIDER: HOMESTYLES
PUBLISHING AND MARKETING
ENTRYWAY DESIGN: TIMOTHY THOELECKE JR.,
APLD, ASLA, GARDEN CONCEPTS, INC. & BRUCE
BURCH, BURCH, BURCH, & BURCH, AIA, LTD.

Before/After

Changes to this ranch-style house include shutters at the windows and railing and trim around the front porch. A gable above the front door helps identify the entry to the home. New paneled garage doors combined with a circular window centered above the doors enlivens this aspect of the house. Planting beds are added along the front of the house and along the widened stone walkway and wooden railing that lead guests from the lawn and driveway. Finally, a mid-sized tree is added on the left side of the lawn to balance the tree on the right.

ENTRYWAY MAKEOVER: TRADITIONAL HOME

The entryway to the traditional home at right was transformed in several key ways: First of all, plantings in the form of ground covers, perennials, annuals, and mid-sized shrubs fill in the barren front yard. Plantings are symmetrical near the steps; asymmetrical balance is achieved further from the steps with a large shade tree beside the pathway and a mid-sized ornamental tree to the left of the house. All the plantings add color and variety to the entryway.

New windows, including a circlehead window above the uppermost unit, and a new front door impart a look of quality to the home. A new rail and posts on the porch give the entryway a stately air. Coach lights on either side of the door match the traditional flavor of the home and complete the look.

Latticework and raised planters below the porch complement the porch rail and the dentil molding of the facade and give the structure a feeling of unity. Green shutters, which match the greenery added to the yard, help to create a feeling of unity between house and landscape. A landing, in the form of one deep step level with the top of the planters, contributes to this effect.

Finally, the siding was changed from an unattractive powder blue to a neutral beige, helping to make the house more friendly and approachable.

ENTRYWAY DESIGN: TIMOTHY THOELECKE JR., APLD, ASLA, GARDEN CONCEPTS, INC. & BRUCE BURCH, BURCH, BURCH, & BURCH, AIA, LTD.

Before/After

Changes to this home include new windows and a new door. Columns, coach lights, porch railing, and latticework were added along with dentil molding and shutters. Roofing and siding color were also changed.

Planting beds, including raised beds adjacent to the porch, are other new additions. A landing was built on to the steps, while the concrete walkway has been changed to flagstone.

SMALL IMPROVEMENTS WITH BIG IMPACT

Not every improvement to your home's entryway has to be an all-encompassing, costly enterprise with contractors, painters, and assorted professionals on call. There are lots of little things you can do to spiff up your home's curbside appeal that don't require a lot of money or time. And if done carefully, these minor changes can have a dramatic effect.

In this chapter, we'll offer some suggestions for adding a touch of beauty, style, and color to your entryway. Most are things you can do on your own. So if you are searching for a new look for your home—without the accompanying big budget—these ideas are for you.

Beginning on page 35, we'll outline the easy way paints and stains can add color and charm to your home. Economical additions—such as architectural moldings and cupolas—are discussed beginning on page 37. Some finishing touches that will perk up first impressions of your home—from mailboxes to door knockers—are detailed beginning on page 41. Finally, for tips on keeping your lawn and home's exterior neat and clean throughout the year, turn to page 43.

This rustic variation on a traditional window box brightens the facade and brings flowers closer to eye level. To construct it, pliable grapevine was wired to a metal form, then filled with a purchased liner and soil.

NEAT AND TRIM

With a few spare hours, an eye for color, and some inexpensive materials, you can add new life to your home with strategic strokes of paint. In almost no time at all, you can perk up old or weather-beaten window trim, shutters, porch columns, railings, and other exterior details.

Freshly painted trim makes a house look neat and well cared for, and, by selecting a popular color, you can make an older house look more modern. But keeping trim painted is more than just a matter of looking good. Paint seals out the weather and protects wood. Once the paint begins to crack and peel, water and sun can quickly cause warping and rot. By painting periodically, you help ensure that your house's wood details last. Of course, there's no point in sprucing up the trim if the whole house needs a makeover. Turn to page 52 for information on redoing the entire exterior.

If your house's trim is stained rather than painted, it's just as important to restain periodically. You can also decide to paint trim that previously has been stained. Unfortunately, it's usually not possible to do the opposite—stain trim that previously has been painted—because it's difficult to remove all traces of the paint.

Whether you're painting or staining, you'll need to first prepare the surface. If the surface is in good condition, simply wash it down. Any existing paint that is cracked or peeling must be removed. The most common way to remove old paint is with a paint scraper. The paint that doesn't come off can be painted over; use sandpaper to feather the edges. This job is most suited to straight and flat surfaces with no ornamental detailing. Although this method can be time-consuming, it yields good results. Be careful not to damage the wood by gouging it with the point of the scraper.

An electric paint remover is another means to remove old paint. Resembling a hair dryer, this hand-held tool directs high heat at the surface, forcing the paint to lift; the lifted paint is then removed with light passes of the

Wide eaves and doric columns, plus the red-and-green trim that complements the lush Florida landscaping, lend a distinctive air to an attractive home that recalls traditional islands architecture.

scraper. Although less labor-intensive than simple scraping, this method requires time and patience as it is most effective in small areas at a time. To avoid breathing in the fumes of the heated paint, wear a cartridge-type respirator and select the cartridge designed for use with chemicals such as paint.

If you're dealing with smaller, intricate details, such as finely carved porch column caps or railings, you'll probably want to use a chemical paint stripper, available at most hardware stores and home centers. Brushed on the surface with an old paintbrush, paint stripper slowly breaks down the old paint, which is then removed with a clean, dry cloth. Any extra residue can be removed with fine steel wool. You'll need to wear rubber gloves, eye protection, and a respirator with the appropriate cartridge when using this material.

Depending on how the wood was previously finished, you have several options for new finishes, from paints to preservatives to stains. Details on the variety of finishes available can be found on page 52.

Vinyl and vinyl coated products do not take paint well, but some manufacturers may be able to recommend a paint that will adhere to some of these surfaces. For spicing up aluminum or steel extras on your home, brush the surface with a wire brush to remove any flaking paint, clean the surface thoroughly, spot prime any areas where metal is exposed using a good-quality metal primer, and follow with a coat of latex house paint.

In an otherwise subtle color scheme, the black of the front door, porch railings, and windows sashes add a touch of dramatic contrast.

For rustic beauty, nothing beats semitransparent stain applied over unpainted wood. Stain allows the wood's natural character to shine through and won't blister, peel, or chalk.

EASY ELEGANCE WITH ARCHITECTURAL DETAILS

If you feel that your house requires a little something extra to give it the look you're trying to achieve, consider installing one or more of the architectural details on the market today. From the fence to the rooftop, there are affordable and easy-to-install elements that can add a touch of elegance to the front of your home.

Certain elements, such as the columns and moldings shown below, date back to the architectural practices of the Greeks and Romans. Available at home centers and millwork shops today, they can be added to the entryway of your home to give it a more distinctive appearance.

As for window shutters, there is a wide selection from which to choose, including fully functional solid-wood models to plastic imitations that don't open or close. Consider installing them on the front of the house only, where they will be seen from the street.

To add a flourish to your roofline, consider a weather vane, like the one shown on page 39. A weather vane, whether immovable or functional, adds a touch of rus-

tic charm that leads the eye to the roof. Note: Any detailing on your roof needs to be integrated into the home's lightning-protection system. If your home does not have a system, ask your general contractor to suggest a professional who can install one. Awnings, also on page 39, add colorful highlights to a facade while protecting against the elements.

Two contrasting molding styles (left and above) are each distinctive in their own way. The classical-style molding with arched transom was built from a kit, while its rustic counterpart was hand-crafted.

Columns (above) impart the air of a stately manor to any home. The easiest type of columns for installation by a do-it-yourselfer are hollow and surround porch posts. They can be ordered from lumberyards, and come in two pieces.

Shutters give this house (right) a more colorful and eye-catching exterior. They are available in wood, vinyl, or aluminum with movable or fixed louvers, and in a variety of shapes and sizes. Shutters can be ordered from specialty manufacturers and are available at most home improvement and hardware stores. Finish as desired, or leave wood models unfinished to accentuate a rustic motif.

Fanciful wood moldings and stair risers—highlighted by a forest-green and white color scheme—add visual interest to the porch shown below. Moldings are available at millwork shops and some home improvement centers.

Traditional wood finials add a touch of class to the tops of the railing post on the entrance to the home shown above. Finials can be used to add character to fences, gates, railings, posts, arbors, and balustrades.

This entry area, surrounded by a lush green landscape, and topped with a striped bubble awning, is a wonderful spot to greet guests or discuss baseball strategy.

weather vane can add rustic charm to e roofline of a home. Available at ecialty stores, weather vanes can either functional or immovable. The weather ne mounted to the top of the cupola es a Canada goose to show the direc- n of the wind.

Enhance the beauty of ur property with color- ful awnings (below), which can also screen he front of your home from the sun and rain. wnings can be bought a range of styles and olors, in fabric, plastic, or aluminum. Depending on climate, ey can be left up year- und, retracted for the colder months, or dismantled entirely for winter storage.

Gutter systems should either blend in seamlessly with the facade of the house, as above, or stand out as a special decorative element, such as when made of copper (right). While in most cases, gutters won't add much to your house in the way of curb appeal, they are necessary, so some thought should be given to making sure they don't detract from the facade.

Most gutter systems are made of galvanized steel, aluminum, or vinyl. Professionally installed aluminum gutters are often fabricated on site so they'll be seamless, while vinyl systems can be installed by the do-it-yourselfer in just a few hours.

FINISHING TOUCHES

When it comes to creating an attractive entryway, little touches go a long way. Things as diverse as mailboxes, door knockers, and wind chimes are quick additions that require minimal buying power, but will inspire passersby and visitors to take more than a fleeting glance at your home.

As you consider these elements, first look at things as simple as your address numbers. These minor accessories create an impression about your home. Numbers come in a wide variety of shapes and sizes, and are made from everything from solid brass and long-weathering aluminum to rustic wood. You can even choose to light up your entry with illuminated number kits.

Mailboxes come in the standard pouch style—just lift the lid—or in more ornate and original forms. To dress up a rustic summer home, an old-fashioned rural-style mailbox mounted on a post at roadside will do the trick. Whatever style of box you have, make sure it looks like new. If the box is rusted or dented and can't be repaired and repainted, consider purchasing a new one.

Wind chimes and dream-catchers (Native decorations hung by the door that are said to keep evil

These days, mailboxes are designed to add a touch of style or whimsy to a home. The mini-barn shown at far right offers rustic roadside charm. Other examples of nifty mailbox ideas include the antique pickup/flower box (right), and the old-fashioned cast-iron letter box—complete with a Pony Express motif—(middle).

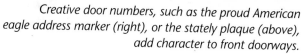
Creative door numbers, such as the proud American eagle address marker (right), or the stately plaque (above), add character to front doorways.

spirits away from the homestead) can be hung from a porch roof, column, nearby tree branch, or above the front door to add a pleasing mystique to any entryway.

Door hardware, including door knockers, lock faceplates, and decorative knobs, are also available in a myriad of styles. Revive old-world style with a hand-carved knocker, which can be catalog-ordered from some suppliers. As well, check out neighborhood antique and thrift shops, as well as garage sale, bazaars, and flea markets—you never know what treasures you might find.

The color and fragrance of flowers and plants can also add style to your entryway. Flower boxes *(below)* or hanging flower baskets are two easy ways to liven up the space. For more information about how plants and planting can add to your curbside appeal, see page 90.

Door hardware serve a practical as well a esthetic purpose. Show above are a few examples antique-style hardware handles, pulls, hinges, an locks. Made from iron, stee or brass, these elegar accessories can be foun at specialty shops or pur chased throug mail-order catalog

Flower boxes brighten up the windowed face of this home. The boxes are pain ed to match the shutters create a harmonious look

QUICK-AND-EASY MAINTENANCE

By staying on top of small-scale maintenance concerns, you'll go a long way toward keeping your house looking great from the curb. The following section presents a few helpful tips and guidelines to keep your home shipshape.

Siding: Siding and roofing can be repaired by replacing affected sections, as shown below and on page 45.

Driveway: If the blacktop surface of your asphalt is starting to look dull and faded, you can improve its appearance simply by recoating it. Inexpensive driveway sealers roll on much like paint, leaving the driveway with the shiny, black look of a completely new surface. Applying the sealer not only improves the look of the driveway, but fills in any hairline

Replacing section of damaged vinyl or aluminum siding

Each piece of aluminum or vinyl siding has interlocking flanges along its edges, and is nailed to the sheathing through slots along one flange. To remove the damaged piece, cut through the center of the panel to just beyond both sides of the damaged area, using a utility knife. Make vertical cuts at both ends, then remove the lower part of the damaged section *(above, left)*. Cut the nailing strip off the replacement by scoring it with a utility knife and snapping it off, then use tin snips to cut this piece so it overlaps

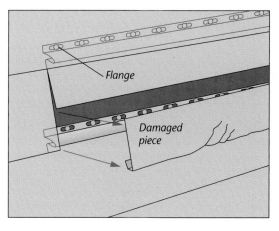

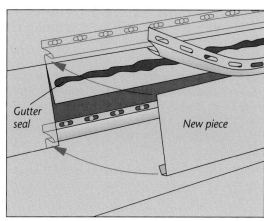

the existing siding by 3" on each side. Apply butyl gutter seal along the nailing strip and press the new piece into place *(above, right)*, hooking the base into the interlocking edge of the section below. Tape or prop until dry.

Repairing section of damaged clapboard-type siding

Mark vertical cutting lines on each side of the damaged area. Pull out any nails in the way of your saw cuts. Pry up the bottom edge of the damaged board with a prybar. Drive small wooden wedges underneath the board at either end outside the cutting lines to keep it raised. With a backsaw, cut through the board along both cutting lines; finish the cuts with a compass saw or a chisel. Break the damaged board out—in pieces, if necessary. Cut any nails passing through the board above with a mini-hacksaw *(inset)*, or pull them out to free the top of the damaged board. Repair any tears in the building paper with roofing cement. Trim the replacement board to length and drive it into position by hammering against a wood block. Nail along its bottom edge, into the sheathing. Caulk or putty the nail holes and board ends; sand, then stain or paint the new board to match the existing siding.

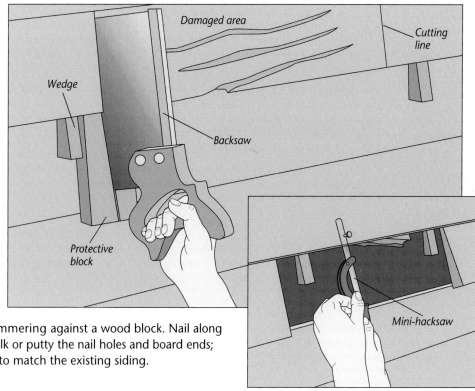

cracks that would otherwise allow moisture to enter and freeze—thus promoting surface deterioration of the driveway.

Concrete and brick driveways can be cleaned with a power washer and coated with a clear sealer. See the tips box below for information on removing tough stains from concrete or brick.

Lawn: Consult a local nursery professional to determine an effective schedule for watering and fertilizing your lawn. Since grass species vary in their growing speed, they require vastly different mowing schedules. The rewards of mowing your lawn can extend beyond the nostalgic smell, look, and feel of newly cut grass. Keeping the lawn trim will help it fend off pests and diseases; avoid cutting it too short as it may shock the roots. For more on lawn maintenance, turn to page 88.

Hedges: Developing a strong boundary of hedges takes considerable planning and care in the first couple of seasons. After that, you can concentrate chiefly on routine maintenance. Prune and shape hedges to follow the winding path of a lawn, or taper and trim their tops and sides so that they are round or flat, or whatever other style fits in your landscape design. For more on caring for hedges, turn to page 91.

Structures: Apart from keeping the lawn, hedges, and garden looking neat and trim, you should also keep siding, walls, walkways, fences, and other structures clean and free of mildew. This is simple with power washers—available to rent or buy at most hardware and gardening supply stores—and commercially available fungicides and mildewcides. Most are safe to use on painted surfaces, but check manufacturer's instructions first.

Slightly more intensive summer chores include repairing minor cracks in walkways and driveways, and keeping steps, stairs, posts, and railings solid and safe. Single fence posts can be easily fixed, or replaced, without much change to the larger, surrounding structure. When the job looks too cumbersome or difficult, consult a professional.

Roof: If you can easily and safely access your roof, it's a good idea to inspect it twice a year—once before winter and once after. Look for broken or damaged units and replace as necessary. Asphalt shingles can be replaced by lifting the shingle above the damaged one with a prybar and prying out the row of nails that holds the damaged one in place. Slide the new shingle into place and—with the tab of the shingle above lifted—nail it to the roof. To replace a shake or wood shingle, follow the steps shown at right. This will help prolong the life of the roof and keep it looking good. Unless you're an accomplished do-it-yourselfer, major repairs to the roof are best left to a professional roofer. (The less walking on the roof the better.)

TIPS ON CLEANING MASONRY

Efflorescence: This white, powdery deposit is caused by the mineral salts in mortar that are dissolved by water, and then appear on masonry, especially brick paving. The salts and deposits will be gone after a few years, but in the meantime, try brushing and scrubbing as much of the deposits away without using water; then follow with a thorough hosing. In an extreme case, follow the directions for removing mortar smears.

Mortar smears: Remove with muriatic acid (available at masonry supply stores), which attacks the alkali in cement and lime. Use a 1:9 acid-water solution on concrete, concrete block, and dark brick. This may stain on light-colored brick, so use a 1:14 or 1:19 solution. Don't use on colored concrete—it will affect the color—or on marble or limestone. CAUTION: When preparing the solution, pour the acid into the water—never the reverse. Wear eye protection, a face shield, and rubber gloves, and work in a well-ventilated area. Wet the wall; then apply acid solution with a stiff brush to a small area at a time, letting it stand for 3 or 4 minutes, then flush with water.

Muriatic acid may change the color of masonry, at least slightly; you may want to treat the whole area to be sure to obtain an even color.

Oil and grease: Before the stain has penetrated, scatter fine sawdust, cat litter, cement powder, or hydrated lime over the surface. These materials will soak up much of the oil or grease and then can be simply swept up.

If the stain has penetrated, try dissolving it with a commercial degreaser or emulsifier. Try to lighten residual stains with bleach, as explained for rust. Avoid solvents such as kerosene, benzene, or gasoline; they are a fire and toxic fume hazard.

Paint: To clean up freshly spilled paint, wipe and scrub it up with a rag soaked in the solvent specified for the paint. Remove dried paint with a commercial paint remover, following the manufacturer's instructions.

Rust: Ordinary household bleach will lighten rust stains (and most others); commercial rust remover is also used. Scrub it in, let stand, then rinse the surface. For stronger stains, use a pound of oxalic acid mixed into a gallon of water; follow the mixing directions for muriatic acid. Brush on the acid, let it stand for 3 or 4 minutes, then hose it off. Remember that acid washes (and bleach) can affect the color of a surface. Test them in an inconspicuous area first.

Smoke and soot: Scrub with a household scouring powder and a stiff brush, then rinse with water.

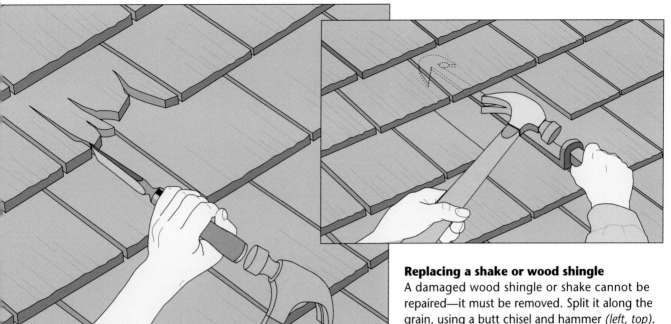

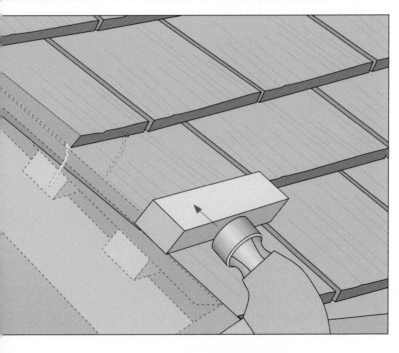

Replacing a shake or wood shingle

A damaged wood shingle or shake cannot be repaired—it must be removed. Split it along the grain, using a butt chisel and hammer *(left, top)*. Pull out as much of the wood as possible, pry up the material directly above the damaged piece, then remove the nails *(inset)* securing it in place with a shingle ripper—which you can rent—or use a mini-hacksaw. Trim the new shingle or shake with a saw, keeping a $1/4$-inch clearance on each side for expansion, then insert it so it protrudes about $1/4$ inch below the adjoining units. Drive in two roofing nails at an angle, just below the edge of the row of shingles or shakes above. Finally, drive the edge of the new shingle or shake even with the other shingles, using a hammer and wood block *(left, bottom)*.

Gutters: Remove leaves, twigs, and other debris from gutters on a regular basis; wear leather work gloves to protect your hands and always work from a sturdy ladder with a helper supporting it at the base.

Loosen dirt with a stiff brush; then hose down the gutter trough to clean it. Clean out blocked downspouts with a garden hose. For stubborn blockages, feed a drain-and-trap auger into the downspouts and then flush out debris with a hose. Add mesh screens over your gutters to avoid future obstructions.

Clean and patch any leaky joints or holes in gutters. Seal pinholes with a dab of roofing cement. For larger leaks, apply silicone sealant to the seams where gutter sections and connectors meet. Seal both the inside and outside of the gutter. If a section of your gutter system is badly damaged, replace it immediately so roof runoff doesn't damage the siding.

Windows: If you have a wooden-framed window that sticks, the problem may be as simple as a dirty or newly painted sash sticking to the molding. Remedy the problem by sanding the troubled area.

The problem may instead be that the channel has narrowed over time. Widen it by tapping a wooden block slightly wider than the channel itself against the stop. The window should soon slide up and down easily.

YOUR HOME'S BEST FACE

First impressions are important—for people and for the curb appeal of homes. As for the latter, it's key that the front of your home displays the best possible look that time and budget allow in order to make the right impression on visitors and neighbors.

From adding a porch to altering your roofline or changing the color of paint, there are many ways—some very involved, some less so—to improve the look of your home's facade. If inspiration is what you need to get started, try visiting local home centers that feature home exteriors, displaying products and ideas. Better yet, plan a "site-seeing" tour of your neighborhood, and note the most interesting motifs you find. You're sure to come across something that piques your interest.

This chapter is intended to help kick-start your imagination as you consider making changes and improvements to the front of your home. In it, you'll find a wide range of ideas and some useful information on siding, porches, and roofing. There's even a section on choosing the best possible paint or stain.

Many different elements combine to give this home its best face, from the columns of the portico to the shutters on the windows and the balustrade surrounding the cupola.

SMART SIDING

Whether protecting your home or defining its style, siding comes in many forms and decorative options. From clapboard to wood shakes or stucco, the face of a home is often defined by this most basic of elements. The chart below provides insight into various siding materials.

Before planning a major overhaul of the siding on your home, take time to decide upon the most attractive and appropriate material for the job. In general, a traditional appearance can be achieved with clapboard, wood shakes or shingles, or stucco. Vinyl or aluminum are made to look like wood. Thinking your choice through is a wise investment in time—once the siding is installed, you'll have to live with it for a long time.

On the level-of-difficulty scale, installing siding deserves a pretty high rating, although some are easier to install than others. Apart from esthetics—finishing off around doors and windows can be quite tricky—siding acts as the outer skin of your home. For this reason, hiring a professional to do the job is a good idea. A contractor has all the right tools and techniques to ensure that the job is done right and the siding is

Clapboard siding combines with conventional and decorative shingles to create an interesting facade (above). Different colors highlight the various elements.

weather-tight, important when you consider that it's the first line of defense against the elements.

We'll explore siding in greater detail over the following pages so you can make an informed decision on this very important element of your home's facade.

A LOOK AT SIDING

Type	Cost	Characteristics	Finish	Upkeep
Aluminum	Inexpensive to moderate	Extruded panels; horizontal panels simulate 6" and 8" wide lap boards; vertical panels simulate 8" wide boards with battens.	Wide range of factory-baked colors. Can be refinished with paint recommended by manufacturer.	Needs annual hosing off. Clean surface stains with nonabrasive detergent.
Artificial masonry veneer	Moderate to expensive	Manufactured to look like stone; lighter in weight. Comes in wide range of textures and colors.	Clear waterproof finish enhances natural look.	Clean to remove dust or dirt.
Brick veneer	Moderate to expensive	Varies in appearance from region to region; a few common appearances include smooth, matte, speckled, and used.	Prefinished; usually left unpainted and untreated.	Clean to remove dust or dirt.
Hardboard	Inexpensive to moderate	Available smooth or in textures including rough-sawn board, stucco, and many others.	Can be painted or stained after board ends have been sealed.	Clean to remove dust or dirt; repaint every 3 to 7 years.
Plywood or oriented strand board (OSB)	Inexpensive to moderate	Available in wide panels or narrow boards. Textures range from smooth to rough-sawn.	Can be painted or stained after panels are installed.	Clean to remove dust or dirt; repaint every 3 to 7 years.
Steel	Expensive	Extruded textured panels simulating cedar shakes; comes in a wide range of colors.	Factory-baked paint.	Needs annual hosing off; repaint scratches to prevent rust.
Stone veneer	Expensive	Comes in many decorative shapes and patterns.	Unfinished or coated with clear waterproof finish.	Cleaning to remove dust or dirt; check for minor cracking.
Vinyl	Inexpensive	Same as aluminum; broad range of colors.	Factory finish; avoid repainting.	Occasional cleaning to remove dust or dirt.
Wood shingles and shakes	Expensive	Small units offer natural, rustic, or traditional appeal.	Can be stained or painted.	Clean to remove dust, dirt, or mildew; replace damaged units as necessary.

WOOD SHINGLES

Available in a variety of specialty designs, shingles also double as roofing materials. Usually cut from cedar or pine, shingles offer rustic appeal while adapting well to curved walls and intricate architectural styles.

Shingles are primarily sold without a finish, but are also available prestained or painted. Like all wood products, they are flammable, although some are sold pretreated with a flame retardant. As well, sidewall shakes—shingles that have been given deep, machine-grooved faces, parallel edges, and straight ends—are available unfinished or preprimed with paint. See your local dealer or visit a home center for more information.

Although they are relatively easy to work with, shingles can take a long time to install because they are small. However, any small-scale damage can usually be handled quickly by prying up the affected units and replacing them with new ones.

The rounded ends of these specialty shingles he offset the front door from the straight solid boar siding on the rest of this hom

While the first floor facade combines brick and siding cedar shingles are the order of the day across the exterior of the second floor. The shingles are painted the soft green of the trim to unify the two stories.

Shingles come in different shapes and size While it's easier to purchase standard cu (below, far right), unique patterns such as th others shown can be specially ordere

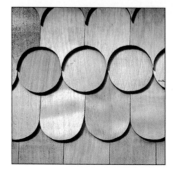

OLID BOARD AND PLYWOOD SIDING

olid board siding—including clapboard, board-on-board, nd board-and-batten—is available in many species, ncluding redwood and cedar. It may be applied horizon- lly, vertically, or diagonally, depending on the type. It kes a wide range of finishes, and provides a small mea- ure of insulation.

Plywood is less expensive than wood boards, yet can ffer the same type of classic appearance. Some panels an serve as both sheathing and siding, adding struc- ural support and strength to walls. The Engineered Vood Association's APA 303 siding is a good example f a plywood that offers structural integrity and esthetic ppeal. It comes in many different wood species and

with various surface textures, from rough or resawn to smooth overlay for painting. And depending on the effect you want to create, you can choose from a vari- ety of patterns, including reverse board-and-batten and channel groove. Most plywood siding is designed to perform best with stain finishes.

Of all the siding types available, the installation of plywood may be the most manageable, provided there is a good nailing surface. Because of the tricki- ness of finishing around doors and windows, and at corners, it is still best to hire a professional. Maintenance and minor repairs can be handled by the do-it-yourselfer.

Painted plywood siding gives the front of this home a bright appearance. This type of siding comes in various textures and patterns.

The painted siding on the home shown at left helps give it a classic American look. Comprising one of the most common categories of solid board siding, clapboard is available in all standard board sizes, surfaced or rough.

VINYL, ALUMINUM, AND STEEL

The white aluminum siding on this home gives the facad a bright appearance. Aluminum will hold its brightnes longer if a regular maintenance schedule is followed. It ca be repainted when the finish fades

Vinyl and aluminum sidings are long-lasting materials that can bolster curb appeal with a moderate investment. As a bonus, aluminum and vinyl can be installed by accomplished do-it-yourselfers. Steel, a considerably more expensive option, is best left in the hands of a professional for installation.

There are several advantages to adding any of these three to the front of your home. In general, they offer an attractive finish that will withstand the elements much more effectively than wood sidings. Over time, this translates into less time and money invested in maintenance. The materials may also increase the energy efficiency of your home.

Of the three, vinyl siding may be the easiest to install and the best suited to withstand denting and scratching. Its drawback is that it may not hold a new coat of paint well—something to consider when it comes time to change the color of your siding.

Aluminum siding—more rigid than vinyl but considerably softer than steel—is also easy to work with. You can cut it yourself fairly readily, so it's easy to make your own repairs. Aluminum is prone to suffering damage in shipping, and its use has diminished greatly, but it remains popular in certain areas of the country. Unlike vinyl, it can be repainted quite easily.

Steel siding comes in many colors, and in smooth and wood-grain textures. It is resistant to denting, and is used primarily in areas of the country that experience large-sized hail on a regular basis. It's best to have a contractor install steel siding, unless one has above-average skills—steel is difficult to handle and cut. As well, it rusts where the surface is scratched, and may corrode near salt water.

Far from looking artificial, vinyl siding (above) imparts the look of wood at less expense and with less maintenance. It's an easy and inexpensive way to add curb appeal to a home.

BRICK, STONE, AND ARTIFICIAL MASONRY VENEERS

Brick, stone, or artificial masonry veneers can add a touch of elegance to a home. As well, these siding materials are long-lasting, low maintenance options that often increase the value of the property.

Due to their high price tags, however, brick, stone, and artificial masonry may not be the first siding choice for many homeowners; each requires the services of a professional for installation. Stone also requires that the foundation footings be strong enough to withstand the weight of the wall.

Suppliers carry many shapes and sizes of stones and textures of brick. It's best to look at a sampling before making your decision. Although less weather-resistant than actual masonry, artificial masonry veneer is less expensive and more readily available in a wider variety of styles. It is manufactured from concrete designed to resemble real masonry.

The bricks on the home above— from the facade to the side walls to the steps— give it its character. Brick acts as a good outer shell for a home, weathering well and requiring little maintenance.

The stone walls of this home lend a solid and rich appearance to the facade. The most difficult and expensive veneer to install, stone is also the most durable.

FINISHING WITH PAINTS AND STAINS

The easiest—and often most noticeable—change to your home's face can be accomplished with the stroke of a paintbrush. Paints and other finishes can be applied to most sidings, porches, and exterior surfaces to protect, preserve, and add a touch of flair.

The two main types of exterior finishes are latex (water base) and alkyd (solvent base or oil base). Latex products are less harmful—both to people and the environment—than alkyds. The chart below will help you select the paint or stain best suited for your house. For quick reference when working on a particular surface feature, see the chart at the bottom of page 53.

Paints: Paints offer uniform coverage in a choice of colors to match your house. Latex paints are available in as wide a range of colors and finishes (flat, semigloss, and gloss) as alkyd paints, and will perform slightly better—some siding manufacturers recommend against using alkyd paints. A good-quality latex paint lasts about five years.

Stains: An alternative to paint, stains are an attractive choice, especially for decorative shakes and shingles. Stains are generally available in two color intensities. Semitransparent types tint the wood, but won't hide the natural grain. Solid-color stains (also called heavy-bodied, or opaque, stains) contain more pigment; many are almost as opaque as paint. Some manufacturers offer a third option: transparent stains with subtle amounts of color. These are intended for use with attractive, naturally decay-resistant wood products, such as cedar shingles; they tend to enhance or intensify the color of the wood while providing extra protection from weathering.

Application: Use a brush or roller rather than a sprayer (sprayers require practice for effective use). The job may be time-consuming, but these tools are inexpensive, precise, and easy to use.

Match the brush type to the desired finish: synthetic bristle brushes are suitable for most types; use natural bristle brushes only with alkyd paints. The better the brush quality, the better the finish. For rollers, the nap thickness needed depends on the texture of the sur-

OUTDOOR COATINGS AND THEIR SUITABILITY

Interior/Exterior Paints	Qualities and Advantages	Specifics and Disadvantages
A. Latex masonry	Durable, quick drying, easy application and cleanup. Water thinned. Nonyellowing.	May not adhere well over coats of oil/alkyd paint.
B. Powder cement base	Least expensive masonry paint. Can be applied to any unpainted or similarly painted porous masonry surface (like stucco).	Must be mixed with water beforehand; pastel colors only.
C. Trim enamel	Glossy, hard enamel finish. Stain and chip resistant. Buy in quart cans or spray containers.	Must prime bare surfaces before application; used for trim.

Exterior Paints and Stains	Qualities and Advantages	Specifics and Disadvantages
D. Oil/alkyd house paint	Oil or alkyd base. Solvent thinned. Bright colors. Acts as vapor barrier.	Slow drying. Use restricted in some regions due to pollution from evaporating solvents as paint dries. Yellows.
E. Latex house paint	Can be modified acrylic or vinyl emulsion water-base. Dull or semigloss finish. Highly resistant to damage. Easier to apply and clean up than oil-base. No fire hazard. Nonyellowing.	Substrates may bleed through paint.
F. Exterior trim	High gloss. Hard, durable surface. Available in oil and alkyd base and latex base. Latex can also be used on brick, concrete, or asbestos shingles. Excellent color retention. Durable.	Latex trim quicker drying than oil-base trim.
G. Shingle	Available in oil or alkyd resin base, and latex base. Shouldn't blister or peel. Latex coating breathes.	Latex variety may need special primer.
H. Deck/porch enamel	Oil or alkyd base. Excellent adhesion to floor and abrasion resistant.	Must be thinned with solvent. May be susceptible to deterioration on concrete because of alkalies or excess moisture.
I. Exterior wood stains	Natural wood finish available in semitransparent or opaque. Special shingle stain available. Oil, alkyd, or latex base. Penetrates and stains wood. Won't peel, blister, or chalk.	Use with sealer on new surface or previously stained surface.

The photo at right shows just how bright an entryway can be with a good coat of paint. The cheerful yellow of the siding is accentuated by the bright white trim work. The white extends down to the fence and greets visitors as they approach the house. To keep your house looking this good, plan to paint every five to seven years.

face to be covered. Use a thick nap for heavily textured surfaces, such as shakes, and a thin nap for smooth surfaces, such as untextured plywood siding.

Cover the surrounding area with drop cloths. Use the paint roller with care to avoid splatters. With a brush, gently lift it away from the surface at the end of each stroke. Smooth surfaces require less paint than textured, and some surfaces absorb more stain than others; read product labels for approximate coverage.

Solving exterior paint problems: There are many causes of paint damage on exterior wood surfaces. Before repainting, find the cause of the problem to prevent future occurrences.

Typical causes of paint damage include improper surface preparation, careless painting, and structural problems that trap moisture in the wood. **Blistering** occurs when water or solvent vapor is trapped under the paint. Bare wood underneath a cut-open blister signifies a water blister caused by moisture escaping from damp wood. Paint underneath it indicates a solvent blister, caused

by painting in sunlight or on wet wood. **Peeling** occurs when paint is applied over dirty, greasy, or wet wood, or over loose paint. **Alligating**—a checkered pattern of cracks resembling alligator skin—results when a top coat is applied before the bottom coat is dry, or when the coats are incompatible. If paint is applied too thickly, **wrinkling** is the result. Although exterior paint is designed to chalk so rain will clean dirt from the surface, an unprimed surface, or one with low-quality paint, will yield **chalking,** which rubs off.

Wood surfaces must be clean, dry, and in good condition before repainting. Repair damaged pieces, and fix any structural damage that will allow water to penetrate. Remove dirt and damaged paint with a stiff wire brush, paint scraper, or pressure washer. With severe paint damage, remove it down to the bare wood. Feather the edges of any remaining paint with medium-grade sandpaper, then sand again with fine-grade sandpaper. If the top coat didn't adhere to a previous coat, rough up the damaged paint with sandpaper. Wash greasy or very dirty wood with a mild detergent, hose it off, and let it dry thoroughly before painting.

For moisture problems, apply a water repellent, then a prime coat; cover with two coats of high-quality paint after preparing the surface.

Prevent water penetration with a clear waterproofing sealer applied to the ends of wood boards. Brush a prime coat on bare or new wood. Heat and humidity can cause wood to deteriorate—treat boards with a wood preservative before sealing.

Not all woods are protected with paint and stain. Redwood, cedar, and southern red cypress need only to be sealed to help retard color changes. Use a finish that is a close match for the existing one.

Paint exteriors in fair, dry weather with temperatures between 50° and 90°F. Wait until the morning dew has evaporated and stop before evening dampness sets in.

OUTDOOR SURFACE	APPROPRIATE PAINT/STAIN
Asbestos shingles	E, F, G
Brick	A, E, F
Concrete block	A, B, E
Eaves	D, E, F, I
Metal trim	C, D, F
Stucco	A, B, E, F
Wood decks, porches	D, H, I
Wood shingles and shakes	G, E, I
Wood siding	D, E, G, I
Wood trim, doors, frames	D, E, F, I
Wood trim, window frames	C, D, E, F, I

PLEASANT PORCHES

A porch is the sort of feature that can improve the front of a home in several key ways: it provides shelter at the front door, adds a touch of nostalgia to the facade of the home, and helps link the home to the neighborhood, as homeowners and visitors alike use the space for relaxing and visiting.

Whether it is simple and rustic in design *(right)*, or modern and trendy *(below)*, it's important that the porch suit the style of your house.

Wraparound porches—which extend from the front of your house around the corner along the side wall—can increase your outdoor entertaining area substantially. Columns, railings, screens, and ceilings are all finishing touches you might want to consider. All of these features can be added on to an existing porch, or can be built with a new one.

Fit for rocking and relaxing, the porch o the front of this rustic home is simple i design and features commonly availabl construction materials. The wood floorin is spaced with slight gaps to allow fc moisture runoff and expansior

Instead of a railing, the porch at left makes use of plantings to define its borders. Pairs of twin columns rising from a masonry deck support the roof. Casual furniture completes the tranquil setting—making it attractive to both man and beast.

The warm glow of lights on this front porch invites neighbors for a twilight visit. Lush plantings bordering the deck of the porch add to the tranquil setting.

The simple yet tasteful porch at right extends the entire width of the front of this home. The railings and posts e painted to match the trim on the windows and doors, creating a harmonious effect.

The bright finish and decorating accessories on the porch at left (inset) go a long way toward creating a cheerful setting. The small open area extends to a larger, closed porch on the other side of the screen door.

Adding a Porch

A well-constructed porch will add style, prestige, and value to your property by providing additional space for outdoor entertainment and relaxation while adding to the overall look of the front of the home. An example of a home pre- and post-porch is shown below.

Unless you are an accomplished designer and builder, planning and building a porch is a major undertaking—one best left in the hands of a competent professional.

There are several details to consider in the planning stage of any new addition. Go over these with your contractor or architect so that you're both fully aware of all the work—

and corresponding expense—that will be required.

One of the main points to keep in mind is that the new addition should be appropriate for the style of the home; this is largely the domain of an architect.

Using the rules of style, scale, color, proportion, and configuration, an architect can design a new porch so that it is in harmony with the existing structure. The ultimate goal of the design is to make it difficult to discern exactly what is existing and what has been added.

An architect's plans will also ensure that the porch doesn't have a negative impact on interior spaces, like

blocking views and light. Support columns can be situated away from windows and skylights installed in the roof, for example.

Before it's time for construction, a contractor will ensure that the land that will support the new addition is ready to build on. One important point includes checking the slope of the lawn to make sure it doesn't rise more than 3 feet in 12 (the land will have to be professionally excavated if it does). Also, a contractor should ensure that there are no underground utility lines that will interfere with the placement of concrete footings needed beneath pier supports.

A neighbor-friendly front porch is the perfect addition to this simple ranch-style house. The house prior to the porch (right), is definitely not as welcoming, as the main entrance is lost in the facade.

ROOFING OPTIONS

A roof does more than provide a weathertight cap on a house. It's also a critical architectural feature, blending with and accenting the design of the home and contributing to its overall esthetic impression.

Roofs come in many shapes, from the gable, gambrel, and hip roof, all popularized in 17th-century Europe, to the wall-like mansard roof and flat roof, which have been in use for thousands of years. Changing the roofline (*page 58*) can give a house a whole new appearance.

Apart from the shape of the roof, the material used to cover it helps define the character of a home. Asphalt, wood, and tile (*page 59*) are the three most commonly used materials in residential roofing, although coverings as diverse as galvanized steel and plastic are also used. Other options include stone masonry, slate, aluminum shingles, and metal panels. As you consult with contractors about your options, consider first the appearance of the material. Does it complement or clash with the other architectural features of your home?

Look at the initial cost and ease of application of the roofing material. Also consider the schedule of maintenance required to keep it in tip-top shape. With certain materials, such as slate, availability may be a factor as well. Finally, take into account the longevity of the material. The chart below outlines the possibilities available.

The slate on this roof finishes off the masonry theme of this entryway, providing a visual link with the brick walls and flagstone pathway. Slate offers unmatched permanence, but is not commonly used due to its expensive price.

ROOFING AT A GLANCE

Type	Cost	Advantages	Disadvantages	Upkeep
Asphalt shingles (felt- or fiberglass-base)	Moderate	Available in range of colors, textures. Easy to apply and repair. Conform to roof surface curves.	Brittle in temperatures below 50°F/10°C.	Lasts 12-25 years, depending on sun's intensity; low maintenance.
Concrete and clay tiles	Moderate	Extremely durable; fireproof; come in flat, curved, or ribbed shapes; moderate color range.	Costly to ship, weighty, need sufficient framing, crack when walked on.	Lasts 50+ years. Difficult to install.
Slate	Expensive	Attractive, traditional look. Several colors available. Fireproof.	May become brittle with age.	Lasts 50+ years. Hard to install. Won't deteriorate.
Aluminum shingles	Moderately expensive	Lightweight, fire-resistant, made to resemble wood shakes; moderate range of colors.	Can be scratched or dented by heavy hail, falling tree branches.	Lasts 50+ years.
Metal panels (aluminum or steel)	Varies from inexpensive to expensive	Shed snow easily. Aluminum: Lightweight. Steel: Strong, fire-resistant.	Metal's contraction and expansion can cause leaks at nail holes; noisy in rain.	Durable, lasts 20+ years. Aluminum: Maintenance-free for prepainted panels.
Asphalt (tar) and gravel	Inexpensive	Most waterproof of all materials for low-slope roofs.	Professional must apply it, black surface absorbs heat.	Lasts 10-20 years; hard to locate leaks.
Sprayed polyurethane foam	Inexpensive to moderate	Watertight surface, good insulation; lightweight.	Professional must apply it; sun damage if not coated.	Lasts for life of building with proper maintenance.
Wood shingles and shakes	Moderate	Appealing natural appearance; durable.	Flammable unless treated with fire retardants; time-consuming application.	Loosens and requires renailing; becomes brittle; lasts 20 years.

ROOFLINE IMPROVEMENTS

The peaks and spires above the added-on bay windows of this home lend strong character to its roofline. The small peaked roof covering the entryway is a continuation of the theme created above.

Overhanging eaves with exposed beam—a trait of the Old Florida architecture that inspired this home—are repeated in the dormers and peaks of the roof.

The simple peak above the half-circle window interrupts the straight run of this roofline, creating a pleasing view. Architectural molding added to the apex of the peak adds to the charm.

ROOFING MATERIALS

The three most popular forms of roofing materials are asphalt shingles, wood shingles, and clay and concrete tiles. A brief description of each, along with corresponding photos, is offered here.

Asphalt shingles: Asphalt shingles are economical, attractive, widely available, and easy to install and maintain. Organic-base shingles have felt mats and are commonly known as asphalt or comp shingles. Fiberglass-base shingles have a fiberglass mat as the base.

Most asphalt shingles have built-in wind protection because they are made with a self-sealing mastic that welds neighboring tabs together after they are installed.

Shapes range from the regular rectangular butts, which give a roof a clean, smooth appearance, to random-edge butts that provide a rustic look. Premium-weight shingles have a three-dimensional look comparable to that of wood shingles. Specialty types—such as T-lock or Dutch lap shingles—are available in some areas.

Wood shingles: Shingles and shakes are an attractive, durable roofing option; be sure to specify Number 1

The big three types of roofing materials include asphalt shingle (above), wood shingle (below, left), and clay or concrete tiles (below, right). Although varying in style and price, each provides durable protection.

grade wood. This grade requires that the wood be all heartwood (the most durable, sap-free part of the tree) and straight-grained. Specialty shingles have a shape—rounded or angled

to a point, for example—cut on the ends that will remain visible. Shingles and shakes are usually installed by a professional; both are also used as siding. For more information on wood shakes and shingles, turn to page 48.

For more information on wood shakes and shingles, turn to page 48.

Clay and concrete tiles: Until recently, classic red-clay roofing tiles—barrel-shaped and made to last the life of the building—were an exclusive highlight of Mediterranean and Spanish-style homes. They are a familiar feature of architecture influenced by early Spanish settlements. But with the introduction of equally durable concrete tiles, roofing tile usage has flourished.

Available in a variety of shapes—including flat, ribbed, S-shaped, and textured—tiles are nailed or fastened with wires. Others come with interlocking edges. Concrete tiles can be found in a spectrum of colors—from earth tones to shades of blue, red, green, and black. They can be heavy, however, and your house will need additional structural bracing.

APPEALING DOORS AND WINDOWS

Doors and windows are a home's connection between indoors and out. As such, they communicate a great deal about the quality of a home. If these features are well made and esthetically pleasing, they will accent the home design and help ensure the overall impression of the entryway is a good one. Unattractive doors and windows, on the other hand, will compromise everything around them.

If you're considering changing your doors or windows, it's a good idea to consult an architect to make sure the new ones will match the architecture of your home. Several door types are shown on page 62. Window styles are discussed starting on page 65.

Alternatively, there are some small steps you can take to spruce up these elements at little cost. A door can be given a fresh look—and an added level of security—with a shiny new lockset. For ideas on beautifying the biggest door on the house—the garage door—see page 63. As for windows, replacing a sash on a double-hung unit *(page 67)* will save you the money you might otherwise have spent buying a replacement. Other ideas for improving the appearance of your windows are given starting on page 65.

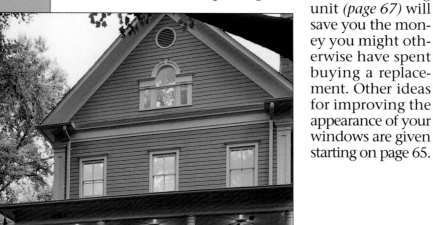

In a new house, a Palladian-style window in the third story and a charming doorway with sidelights and transom create a striking, yet simple facade in harmony with its Queen Anne ancestors.

DISTINGUISHED DOORS

The front door is like a homeowner's ambassador to the outside world. It adds insight into the style and taste of the occupant, while welcoming friends and strangers alike.

How you dress up your front door will depend partly on what type it is. Most front doors are either panel or flush types. Panel doors have solid vertical stiles and horizontal rails, with flat or raised panels in between. Flush doors are flat and built from skins of wood, steel, or composites attached to a solid wood or foam core. Many entry doors have glazed openings called lights. A selection of door types is shown on page 62.

Existing doors can be beautified with a new coat of paint (always sand or strip the surface before painting).

If you have a panel door, consider painting the area around each panel in an accent color. For flat doors, you can add interest with carefully applied molding to bring about a paneled effect. Buy the molding at a lumberyard, then use an existing panel door to guide you in putting it on.

Also consider the details and accessories that define the doorway. Attractive doorbell fixtures, door knockers, house numbers, mailboxes, and wind chimes *(page 41)* all help make the door the focal point of the front of your home.

If you're considering replacing the front door, you'll find a wide selection of new doors at many lumberyards and home improvement centers.

A transom combined with sidelights beautifully set off a classic paneled door. The sidelights allow occupants to see guests outside the door and let natural light into the home's entry.

First and foremost, make sure the door you choose matches the architecture of your home. The market is aimed at replacements for existing doors, so you will likely find what you need; if not, doors can be custom-made in any style, from simple and traditional to highly decorative.

Even if you choose to have the door installed by a professional, it will help to have some idea how it's done. Doors come in either prehung or standard assembly. Prehung doors come hinge-mounted inside their frame. You simply slide these into the slightly oversize rough opening in the wall, then level and plumb the whole unit. In some situations, you will not be able to use a prehung door. The opening space may not match any prehung units, or you may want a front door that is not available in prehung form.

Installing a standard door can be tricky. You may have to fashion a new door frame to line the rough opening, install molding, or door casing both inside and out to cover the space between the jamb and the wall of the home, and install hinges and hardware. In addition, you may not find a door to fit the opening exactly. In this case, you will have to purchase an oversize door and trim it to fit with a circular saw.

Potted bromeliads frame antique Spanish front doors. The portal around the doors is made of keystone, a native Florida material best described as sliced coral.

Panel   **Flush**   **French**   **Dutch**   **Double doors with sidelights**

GARAGE DOORS

The garage door is the largest single element on the face of many American homes, so it deserves some attention when you consider the entryway as a whole.

There are some simple ways to spruce up a garage door: a fresh coat of paint, wood stain, or even trim colored to match the accents of the front door, window frames, or another architectural detail of the house will work wonders *(page 35)*. You can also give an old door some new life by just changing the hardware *(page 42)*.

If your door is badly damaged or is failing due to old age, you may want to consider having it replaced. You'll be able to choose from several styles—everything from simple flat doors to those that have raised panels, trim, or other decorative details. Most doors are simple to hang. If you choose a roll-up model, you'll need to have a professional install the torsion spring mechanism vital to the safe operation of the door.

Some garage door manufacturers offer inventive styles—such as the vintage design shown in the photo above—which can provide a unique accent to your home's overall architectural theme. These doors are custom-built, so they cost more than other mass-produced models. Custom-built garage doors can be ordered with redwood, fir, or cedar overlays, and then painted to match the house's exterior.

Not all garage doors face front—some are off to the side, or, in unusual cases, at the back of the home. Obviously, garage doors oriented in this fashion play less of a role in the curb appeal of a home. If you're planning on remodeling your home and yard, ask the contractor about the expense and work involved in relocating the garage door to a less conspicuous area, such as the side of the house, or perhaps improving the door's appearance with interesting architectural details, such as trim or moldings.

If you want a bit more personal security when arriving home to your garage, consider installing an automatic door opener. Kits are available at home centers and hardware stores. If you have a central alarm system, you can also have the garage door hooked up to the system.

You'd almost expect a Model T Ford to emerge from this garage. Its arch-topped doors look as though they swing out, like old-fashioned ones. The surprise is that these are sectional doors that lift on the same overhead roll-up hardware used in contemporary garages. **COURTESY: HOLMES GARAGE DOOR COMPANY**

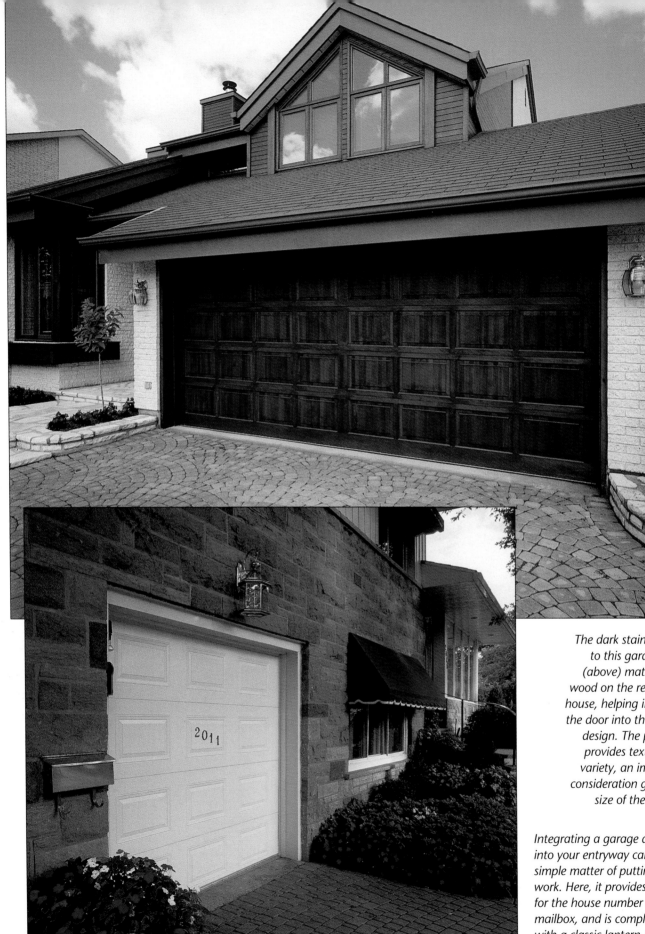

The dark stain applied to this garage door (above) matches the wood on the rest of the house, helping integrate the door into the overall design. The paneling provides texture and variety, an important consideration given the size of the surface.

Integrating a garage door into your entryway can be a simple matter of putting it to work. Here, it provides a place for the house number and mailbox, and is complemented with a classic lantern-style light fixture.

2011

WONDERFUL WINDOWS

Windows are critical elements of your home's entryway, providing architectural beauty, character, and, from indoors, light and views. Like doors, they are focal points, so special attention should be paid to make sure they look their best.

There are several ways to spruce up windows. First, keep the glass clean, and replace any broken panes. The frames, often the first part of a home from which the paint peels, may need to be scraped and sanded and repainted. Another consideration is the architectural elements that surround windows. To add color to your windows, consider installing window boxes with flowers. Keep shutters and other features in top shape. Don't forget to consider the view inside. Many homeowners forget that when the curtains or drapes are open, the inside of the house can be seen from the curb. Keep the sills free of large objects that would block the view to the inside. It's also important, whenever possible, to avoid locating air conditioners or other service units in front windows.

If your windows are in very poor condition, you may be better off replacing them. Windows come in many styles. They can be broadly divided by how they open. Once you've chosen the opening mechanism, you still have to decide on a material—vinyl, aluminum, or wood—a shape, a style of glass, a color, and whether they will project or not. Projecting windows such as angle bay, box bay, and bow windows are discussed on page 66. It is important that any new or renovated windows do not upset the decorative balance of your house. If you are unsure, an architect, designer, or contractor can help you decide beforehand how to use window shapes to your home's advantage. If you require a specific window or style that is not readily available at home improvement centers or window dealers, you can have it custom-made.

Specialty styles: There is a range of specialty window styles that will give your facade a new focal point and added drama. Cathedral and multistory windows, for example, are both characterized by their large size. The

night, light streams outward through dramatic picture windows topped with
half-round accents, giving this home a stunning, almost surreal front facade.

PROJECTING WINDOWS

For a change of pace, projecting windows are a nice way to open up your home to more light. At the same time, an otherwise flat facade will take on depth and added appeal with the introduction of the distinctive outward curves or angles of these traditional window designs.

Greenhouse—or garden—windows are small projecting windows made of metal or wood. Some come with shelves for pots and planters, and are often made to fit standard-size window openings; opening sides or tops help prevent fogging. They can be added to the home, using an existing window opening or by framing a new one. Either way, refer to manufacturer's installation instructions, or have a professional do the job.

Bay windows have a center pane parallel to the wall, flanked by two windows attached at an angle. Bow windows have more than three sections that form a curve. Kits for installing both types of windows are available at home-improvement centers, though inexperienced do-it-yourselfers may want to let a professional handle the task.

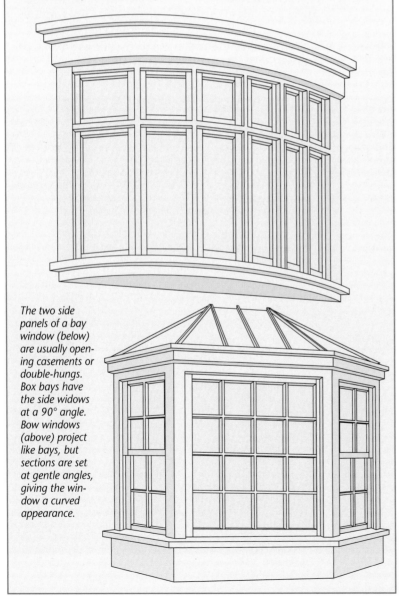

The two side panels of a bay window (below) are usually opening casements or double-hungs. Box bays have the side widows at a 90° angle. Bow windows (above) project like bays, but sections are set at gentle angles, giving the window a curved appearance.

former are intended for parts of the house with very high ceilings; the window generally follow the slopes of the roof and may have vertical divisions. Multistory windows, as their name implies, extend from the ground floor to the floors above with either fixed or opening glass.

If privacy is important, but you don't want to sacrifice style, clerestory windows—which run along the top of a wall near the ceiling—are ideal. Also known as ribbon windows, they allow light to reflect and be refracted from the glass of the window.

Windows are available in a variety of shapes, including octagonal, half-circle, ellipse, trapezoid, and eyebrow. New or renovated windows can also be a focal point of your house's entryway; those with a geometrical shape are especially good for this. A triangular window highlights the angles of a Victorian-influenced home, for example.

Functional style: Sliding windows are those which have a sash that slides either horizontally or vertically. Only half the window can be opened at one time with these windows. Swinging windows impart an open feel to the home. Classic double-casement windows, with two sashes that swing to the outside, allow cooling breezes to enter the house while the absence of a center mullion allows for uninterrupted views in and out. Fixed windows, also called picture windows, cannot be opened. They can be used alone, or in combination with windows with a movable sash. Fixed windows may be glazed with a single large pane of glass or with divided sections.

Glass: Glazed windows can offer increased energy efficiency. Keep in mind R- and U-values when shopping for windows. The R-value is a material's resistance to heat transfer. The higher the R-value, the better the insulating property of the window. The U-value is the best indicator of a window's energy efficiency. It tells you the rate of heat flow through the window; a lower U-value means the window is more energy efficient.

As well, ask a professional about single and multipane windows, and about low-emissivity glass, which is treated to keep your home cool by blocking out some of the sun's rays.

For a different look, consider tinted- or stained-glass windows. A home with colored windows can evoke the feeling of an elegant old-style manor, for example, whereas tinted glass windows afford your home increased privacy with a look more suited to more modern architectural design.

Using Sash Replacements

The traditional look of wooden, double-hung windows has an enduring appeal. However, many old double-hung windows become drafty, inefficient, and unattractive as their sashes are damaged or deteriorate. Few things can detract from a house's appearance like unseemly windows. One cost-effective way to revamp a window is to replace the sash.

A sash replacement kit allow homeowners to change an unsightly or poorly insulating sash by themselves without incurring the cost of hiring a contractor. Kit components can be ordered to custom-fit most frames and styles, and to match your home's existing architectural design. Kits come with all the installation hardware required. A typical installation is shown below.

1 Remove old sash
Remove the stops and the existing window from the frame, and take up all the jamb hardware lining the sides using a prybar.

2 Install new jamb hardware
Fasten metal brackets spaced evenly along both sides of the window (inset). Then install new jamb hardware for the replacement sash. All hardware will be supplied with the kit.

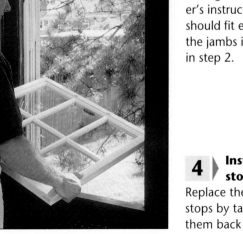

3 Install new sash
Install the new sash in the opening following manufacturer's instructions. It should fit easily in the jambs installed in step 2.

4 Install stops
Replace the existing stops by tacking them back in place.

THE PATH TO YOUR DOOR

A good front path should combine beauty and function, leading visitors from the street to the front door while adding style to your home's entryway as a whole. At the very minimum, the path should complement the house and be well-maintained. A wide variety of front path options are discussed starting on page 69.

Many paths require steps to accommodate the slope of the land, from street level to the front door. As much as the path, steps can set the mood for an entire landscaping scheme. You'll find ideas for steps on pages 72 and 73.

For some homes, the front path incorporates a ramp, sometimes for wheelchair access, other times simply for an easy, gradual climb. Issues of space and materials are primary in planning ramp access. However, like most functional elements in a landscape design, a few finishing touches can tie a wheelchair ramp in to its surroundings. Useful ramp designs are given on pages 74 and 75.

For arrivals by car, a driveway can function as a path. This often neglected entryway element is discussed in detail beginning on page 76.

In a Florida entry, manicured beds of shrubs emphasize the zig-zag shape of the walkway. The pitted concrete path was antiqued with a rock salt finish to blend in with the 1920s architecture of the neighborhood.

FRONT PATH OPTIONS

hink of the front path as an extended welcome mat for the house. To create a good first impression, keep the walkway and lawn or landscaping next to it immaculate. Make sure that there is a clean border between the grass and the path. The paving units should reflect or complement the style of the house. The following pages offer you a few path options to consider.

LOTTING A PATH

you're thinking of changing your walkway, or installing a new one, chances are you'll have a variety f design options. Keep in mind, though, that some f the most attractive walks develop naturally from veryday traffic patterns. You can achieve this effect by simply wandering over your front yard and choosing a route that feels right.

If you're planning a path with a curve in it, a simple way of making the curve look natural is to have the path skirt a focal point in the landscape, such as a large

bluestone walk and front terrace guide visitors to the entry doors. Low stacked-stone walls at reet side and at the terrace unify the sections of the yard.

The front yard above is truly inviting. You enter by stepping onto a wide bluestone landing at the curb, then stroll to the front door, perhaps with a stop to linger at the bench or to admire the planting beds.

tree. If you don't have any such features, you can always plant trees or shrubs in strategic spots and lay out the path so it winds gently past them. To produce an even more interesting result, some landscape designers like to widen the path at the curves.

Flaring the end of a path, whether straight or curved, facilitates traffic. Where space is greater this feature adds elegance and, by directing guests toward the house, conveys a feeling of welcome.

In some cases, a straight front path is the most sensible and least expensive option. A good way to emphasize the lines of a straight path is to create a border with a carefully trimmed short hedge. This reinforces the sense of the path providing a direct route from A to B.

Informal plantings that spill over the edges of the walk will give a straight path a less austere look.

Size, proportion, and slope: Much of walkway design is just common sense. While it's easy to make a front path too narrow, it's rare in a residential design to find one that's too wide. Pathways should be wide enough (4 or 5 feet) to accommodate two or three people at once, and allow comfortable, safe, and easy access. Essentially the path should appear important enough to suggest that it leads to the primary entry (eliminating the possibility that visitors will come to the wrong door by mistake). Whenever possible, a path should slope slightly toward the street so it won't collect water or direct it toward the house and basement.

SELECTING MATERIALS

Keep appropriateness uppermost in mind when you select materials for the front path. As a major accessway it should be made of materials that allow easy traffic flow and provide an even, nonslick surface, such as brick, concrete, unglazed tile, loose materials, or stone.

Brick is a popular choice and is available in varied sizes and colors. Concrete is the most versatile paving material. It can be lightly smoothed or heavily brushed, surfaced with handsome pebbles, swirled, scored, tinted, painted, patterned, or cast into molds that resemble other paving materials. For durability and warmth, nothing can beat stone. Some stone, like flagstone, can be very expensive, while alternatives, like fieldstone and river rocks, are more affordable (their roundness may make them difficult to walk on, however). Loose materials—such as gravel, red rock, or wood chips—provide good drainage and a casual look. They may not be practical in areas that experience heavy snowfall.

Though each paving material has practical advantages and disadvantages, each also has a unique character and has come to be associated with certain types of houses. The photos in this chapter will give you an idea of how some of the most popular materials look when used in front paths.

The deep green of this straight concrete walk blends in with the border plantings. The plants that spill onto the edge of the walk help to soften it. The "green theme" is carried through to the door, windows, and even the trim of the home.

By closely matching the path to the facade, a formal tone is introduced. This is balanced by the curve of the path and the unrestrained garden on either side.

STEP RIGHT UP

The charm of a front yard can be greatly enhanced by garden steps. Wide, deep steps that lead the eye to a garden focal point are particularly appealing (and functional). Such steps can also serve as a retaining wall, create a base for a planter, or provide a place to sit. To soften the edge of a series of steps, as well as to help make them more visible for walkers, place container plants, plantings, or open beds along their borders. On long, straight walks that have just a few steps, changing the surface materials and introducing an unusual step design will add a level of visual interest that would otherwise be lacking.

The choice of possible step designs is enormous, ranging from water-washed stone steps placed to look like a natural outcropping, to colorful concrete steps edged with railroad ties.

Concrete and masonry block units usually present a formal, substantial look. Natural materials such as stone and wood add an informal touch, appearing more at home in a less structured garden.

Constructing the steps from the same material used for the path helps unite a landscape design. Using contrasting materials draws attention to the steps and the parts of the front yard they serve.

To some extent the nature of the steps required will be dictated by the slope of the lawn. For example, on long slopes, the entire path can take the form of a series of wide, "ramp" steps that gently lead the way from the street right to the house. On a very steep property, a long set of steep steps is not the best solution, as such a route is dangerous and uncomfortable to climb and descend. Instead, retaining walls should be used to break up the yard into successive levels that can then be linked with a series of shorter, more manageable sets of steps.

Regardless of the materials and design you choose, put safety first: ensure steps provide safe footing in wet weather, and install adequate lighting (see page 95).

Two sets of steps break a steep rise to the home's front door. Solid walls give way to a steel railing that reveals a shrub. Potted plantings add color to the tops of the other walls.

White Chippendale-style railings set off the warmth of the brick steps and the plantings, including tubs of pink impatiens and the fig vine that covers the risers.

A series of bluestone landings allow guests to ascend to the front door from the drive at a comfortable pace.

RAMPS FOR ACCESS

There are a number of standard ramp designs, notably for wheelchair access, that are appropriate for residential buildings. The right ramp design tends to be dictated by the distance between the entrance and the ground below. For example, a drop of just a foot or two will allow a simple straight ramp. A greater drop will likely demand a ramp that incorporates one or more turns.

When making an entrance accessible, it should be determined if ramps are in fact necessary. It is sometimes possible to grade a slope leading up to a home, eliminating the need for a ramp. Graded pathways, however, should never exceed a slope of 1:20. For their part, ramps should never have a slope steeper than 1:12 (1 inch of rise for every 12 inches of run).

INTEGRATING THE RAMP

A ramp should have a set of stairs next to it to ensure the entrance is part of the common route of travel.

Like stairs, a ramp should be integrated into the existing house design, rather than constructed of completely different materials and details. Plantings and additional landscaping can help integrate the ramp into the surrounding environment.

All materials must be slip-resistant, a critical issue for wood ramps, which can become slippery when wet. Rough-textured concrete is a good choice for a surface material. With concrete's versatility it can be colored or otherwise adapted to suit the existing color theme. Even though it's expensive, it is a good idea to cover the ramp to protect it against the weather, thereby keeping it free of water, snow, ice, and other dangers.

STRAIGHT-RUN RAMPS

Incorporating no turns, a straight run is the most basic ramp design. However, a very long, straight run can be a strong visual element, and may detract from the look of the house. If this is the case an alternate configuration such as a switchback ramp, can minimize the impact on the surroundings.

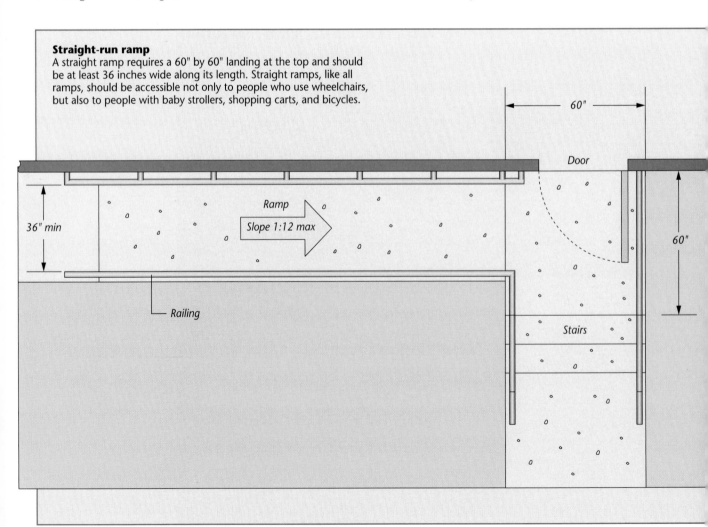

Straight-run ramp
A straight ramp requires a 60" by 60" landing at the top and should be at least 36 inches wide along its length. Straight ramps, like all ramps, should be accessible not only to people who use wheelchairs, but also to people with baby strollers, shopping carts, and bicycles.

60"

Door

36" min

Ramp
Slope 1:12 max

60"

Railing

Stairs

WITCHBACK RAMP

switchback ramp has at least one turn and is a useful
lternative in places where height considerations rule out
straight ramp. Adding an additional ramp length in-
reases the height the ramp can reach. It also enables
ramp to fit into a tighter area than a straight ramp,
naking it useful in situations where there are obstruc-
ons or not enough open land.

ANDRAILS

andrails affect the safety and usability of a ramp as
nuch as the slope and surface material. Handrails pro-
ide an essential gripping surface that enables people with
a range of abilities to use the ramp. Without handrails,
particularly in outdoor locations, ramps are just steep
walkways that can be very difficult and dangerous to use.

Handrails must be designed to provide uninterrupted
support for their entire length on both sides of the ramp.
The diameter of the rail should be from $1^{1}/_{4}$-inch to
$1^{1}/_{2}$-inches diameter. The top of the handrail should
be between 34 inches and 38 inches above the ramp
surface. A $1^{1}/_{2}$ inch clearance is required between the rail
and wall or other surface. On older buildings in particular, rail design should reflect the existing aesthetic by
incorporating color, ornamentation, and other appropriate decorative elements.

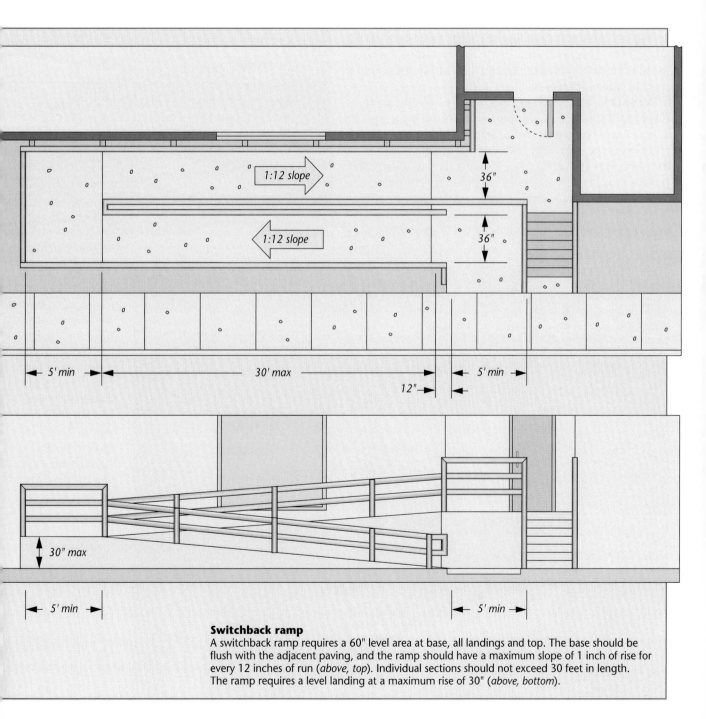

Switchback ramp
A switchback ramp requires a 60" level area at base, all landings and top. The base should be
flush with the adjacent paving, and the ramp should have a maximum slope of 1 inch of rise for
every 12 inches of run (*above, top*). Individual sections should not exceed 30 feet in length.
The ramp requires a level landing at a maximum rise of 30" (*above, bottom*).

DRIVEWAY DECISIONS

When you imagine your dream house, chances are you don't dwell on thoughts of the driveway. Still, there is no reason a driveway can't be an elegant design element and provide ample, easy parking—all it takes is giving some extra thought to paving materials and layout. Since your driveway is one of the single largest features in your front yard, improving its appearance is bound to make a big difference to the look of your property.

Repaving a standard asphalt driveway that has become cracked is a great start. However, if you really want to transform your driveway, consider a less typical surface material. Many of the same paving materials described earlier in this chapter—including bricks, loose materials, concrete, and stone—are increasingly used to pave driveways.

When it's paved with asphalt, there is no mistaking a driveway for what it is. However when the same space is paved with materials that bring to mind patios or pathways, the driveway suddenly seems less one-dimensional and utilitarian (even if its true function hasn't changed). And the extra expense will pay off in an even greater increase in property value.

In addition to the traditional straight design, driveways can take on any number of shapes, depending on

Irregularly shaped concrete pavers make a unique and attractive driveway surface (above). Growing grass between the pavers adds color to a normally drab feature of the entryway. Far from being boring, the concrete driveway (left) matches the retaining wall and steps and complements the home itself.

he site and needs of the homeowner. As the number of arked cars on the street becomes a problem, many peo- le are providing off-street parking for guests, or for their wn cars when not in the garage *(below right)*. To elimi- ate the need to back out onto the street, driveways can lso be adapted to include a turnaround area *(below left)*.

When redesigning a driveway or building a new one, number of basic points should be kept in mind.

Driveways should be a minimum width of 10 feet to ensure they can be negotiated easily by delivery trucks as well as cars. In most cases, long, straight driveways look best when narrower. Driveways that turn must be wide enough to accommodate a car's turning radius. The intended site should be clear of tree limbs and shrubbery that could scratch the exterior of the car.

TWO TYPES OF DRIVEWAY LAYOUT

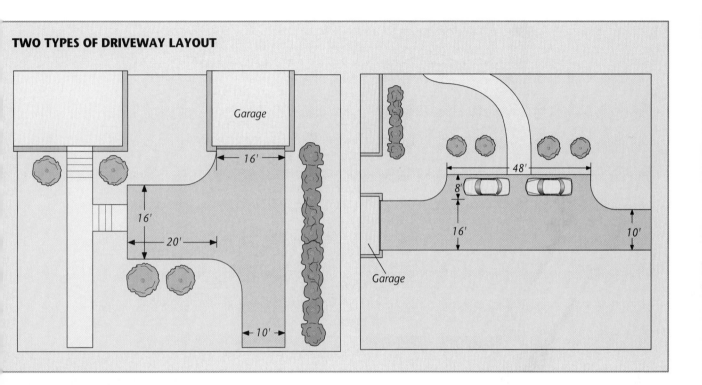

This sprawling park- ing court is made of wire-cut bricks laid in a basketweave pattern atop a concrete slab. Palms and other trees screen just enough of the court to give it a sense of enclo- sure and intimacy.

STEPPING INSIDE

T he entryway to your home comprises more than just the view from the street. Equally important is the first impression that comes just inside the front door. Whether it is a large hallway, a tiny vestibule, or a less-defined space in an open-style layout, the first room that visitors see is the *entrée* to the rest of your house. It must be both beautiful and practical, and it must provide a welcoming starting point for all who enter your home.

To make the most of your entry, you'll need to consider almost all the elements that go into any other room in your home. The walls, ceiling, floor, furniture, and lighting all play an important role in creating a good first impression, as do a selection of other amenities specific to entries, such as hat and coat racks and umbrella stands. The pages that follow contain many ideas for creating an attractive entry. Use them to ensure that your house is just as welcoming inside as it is outside.

Recessed lights combined with an ornate semi-circle of glass, and walls painted deep yellow, impart a soft radiance in this entry. The console table, umbrella stand, and bust on pedestal add a regal air.

DECORATING YOUR ENTRY

There are general guidelines for decorating the entry to your home that may be helpful as you consider making changes. These are not absolute rules, however. First and foremost, the entry should reflect your own personal taste.

Walls are the most prominent element of any entry, so pay special attention to them. Paint is generally preferable for walls, as intricate wallpaper designs can appear too busy in small rooms. Whatever you choose, opt for neutral colors, keeping in mind that any strong decorative element, even boldly colored walls, can cause what designers refer to as "territorial anxiety"—a feeling of uneasiness visitors experience when first stepping into a strange home. Bolder colors can be used effectively as accents and borders, however.

Wall and ceiling moldings, made from wood or precast plastic, are also worth considering for the entry. They are particularly well suited to older homes, where they will impart a traditional character to the space. There are three popular varieties of moldings for the entry: chair rail, picture frame, and cornice. All three can be purchased at lumberyards and home improvement centers.

Paintings and photos will also add interest to the walls of your entry. Again, it's a good idea to avoid hanging or placing your most challenging art here. Stick to more reserved pictures that everyone can enjoy. A mirror will make the space seem larger and capitalize on the existing natural light already in the room. Large wall mirrors should not be located direct-

ly opposite the door. Large framed mirrors go particularly well over a hall table or console.

The floor will also play a key role in determining the look of the entry. Keep wood and tile floors cleaned and shined. To protect the floor and add a decorative touch, consider adding a rug. To keep maintenance to a minimum, opt for dark colored carpet made from durable fibers. If your entry floor is on its last legs, consider replacing it with granite, marble, or flagstone or stone tiles. These materials are not overly expensive when purchased in small quantities, but they will give your home a truly stunning first impression.

When it comes to creating a warm, welcoming atmosphere, lighting also contributes greatly. One ceiling fixture will normally provide adequate light for the entry. Cut-glass or brass fixtures are particularly attractive options for this space. If you need more light, consider adding a table lamp.

A large wall mirror above a marble hall table gives this moderately sized entry hall (above) a spacious air. The wooden bench at left complements the wood motif of the entry and provides a place to sit or temporarily hang coats.

The entry may also require some carefully selected furniture. A wooden chair, a side table, or better yet, a bench with a folding seat and storage underneath are all popular choices that perform practical as well as esthetic functions. Also consider setting up coat and hat racks. Both freestanding and wall-mounted units are available. Antiques are popular, but can be expensive. Handmade wooden units are available in a vast array of styles; shop for the one that best suits your home.

Replace unattractive hardware on front and closet doors. Specialty brass or porcelain doorknobs are not expensive, but they can make a simple door appear very striking. Also keep all hardware and glass in your entry shiny and clean.

Because of the small size of the entry, minor decorative elements will have a major impact. Plants and flowers can be very attractive additions, but only if they are suited to the space and contained in tasteful vases or pots. Replace old switchplates and outlet covers with new brass plates. The small cost will be worth it. A small wooden shelf is also a nice addition to the entry. It can hold a few books, plants or flowers, or small pieces of art.

Finally, if your entry has a closet, spend some time clearing it of clutter. Take anything that does not need to be there to the attic or basement for storage. Buy good-quality hangers for organizing clothing and outerwear. To give the closet a fresh and clean aroma, install an air freshener. Cedar bars or spray will make your closet smell as if it is lined with real cedar wood.

X marks the spot where a jolt of color and a pair of inexpensive louvered doors now make an intriguing focal point for guests entering the home.

In this foyer, handsome wall-mounted lanterns typically used outside by the front door, create an easy transition from exterior to interior spaces. The floor is painted brick; walls are V-groove paneling painted a soft, sandy hue.

Elements in this foyer—a settee, small table, lamps, and hand-painted floor—set an inviting tone for the entry.

The blank wall of an entry foyer was transformed into an instant focal point with a large-scale mirror and sconces. The mirror's oversize dimensions work with the scale of the entry and help set the Country French mood. Beneath the mirror, armchairs upholstered in old kilim rug remnants flank an antique demilune (half-round) table.

Matching red lanterns are the perfect touch for the entry of this rustic home. A small, well-worn wooden bench adds to its authentic charm and provides a place to sit down.

Everything from umbrellas to hats has a place on this attractive coat and hat stand. Complemented by other decorative accessories, it adds much to the look and beauty of the entry.

IMPROVING LANDSCAPING

Landscaping makes a world of difference—and it tells the world a lot about you. The plants and structures that surround your home will reflect your taste, your pleasures, your activities, and your personality.

As the primary element in the curb appeal of any home, the landscape should provide a special lift to visitors striding up the path. And the homeowners who achieve the best results when designing are those who clearly define their goals. In general, the first step will be how to handle the entranceway. Do you want your front yard to be open or private? Do you want the area to be lawn, patio, or ground cover? Do you want to plant a formal or a natural garden?

Of course, landscape professionals can help put your thoughts and ideas into motion. If you're planning on doing some of the work yourself, consider some of the ideas shown over the following pages.

The extensive landscape that fronts this home incorporates trees, shrubs, and flowers. Each of these is discussed in more detail beginning on page 90.

SHAPING THE LAND

Before you set out to shape or reshape the landscape in front of your home, keep in mind the general design principles that should guide your actions *(page 2)*. These, and some advance planning, should produce good results.

One of the basic decisions will be how much of your home to open to the public view from the curb. You can landscape for privacy or for display—or for some of each. Do you have a house whose beauty should be shared with passersby? Do you want to minimize barriers between your property and that of your neighbors? Maybe you'll decide on a public area just large enough to blend with others along the street, while reserving most of the landscape for your private use and enjoyment.

Of course, situations vary from one property to the next. You may want to replace an old landscape with a new overall look. Make the most of this fresh start by boldly altering the basic character of the landscape; you can reshape contours; reroute foot traffic; or make structural changes, such as introducing raised planting beds. Only your imagination and budget set the limits to the approach you'll take.

The landscape of this charming house incorporates a lawn, trees, plants, and shrubs. As an added featured, a boulder acts as a focal point in the view from the curb. This sort of landscape is easy to design and simple to maintain.

If you simply want to give your home's landscape a fast face-lift, there are several quick and easy changes you can make. Thinning back old planting may open up new vistas or make room for a garden, for example. Structural elements may require no more than simple repair and sprucing up. Unlike the homeowner who starts from scratch, you can enjoy all the advantages of a mature landscape instantly, and at little expense.

It is often the case that homeowners decide to keep part of the old landscape and modify the rest. Perhaps your pruning and thinning for a possible face-lift revealed diseased trees or shrubs, or decaying, unappealing features that call instead for a true revision. Homeowners who have successfully revised their landscape follow a basic rule: If a magnificent tree dominates the rear garden, plan the garden around it; but be ruthless in removing features that, even though individually attractive, would make a hodgepodge of the new landscape or limit the scope of planning. Be sure to consider how each change will affect the overall impression.

Obviously, time, effort, and money are important factors to consider when changing any landscape. If for any of these three reasons you can't afford your ideal landscape right away, you needn't settle for an inexpensive, uninspired compromise. Instead, consider landscaping in stages: plan your ideal landscape and decide which features to install now and which to add later. Developing your environment in stages can be more satisfying than doing it all at once.

RETAINING WALLS

The primary function of retaining walls is to hold the earth on sloped terrain in place in time of heavy runoff. They are also used to contain gardens on hilly landscapes. Retaining walls can be made using many different materials, including brick, stone, concrete, interlocking concrete masonry units, dimension lumber, or railway ties.

Other masonry units, such as manufactured concrete and adobe blocks are also suitable materials if reinforced with steel.

The average do-it-yourselfer can handle small walls, although those over 2 feet high require a permit in most municipalities, and anything over 4 feet needs to be designed by an engineer. The easiest way to build a retaining wall is to locate it at the bottom of a slope and fill in behind it with soil. A hill can also be held with a series of low, terraced walls. It is important to add drainage behind retaining walls; with enough water built up behind the wall, it can come tumbling down.

Once your wall is in place, you can improve its appearance with plantings on the surface of the wall itself. For example, a stone wall looks almost like a natural part of the landscape when you work in planting soil and grow plants in the crevices between the stones.

The retaining walls at left in this generous front yard serve a dual purpose: They contain the planting beds and help hide a sunken garden and parking area that sit 4 feet below the lawn.

Water features installed in the front yard can lend both energy and charm to the entryway of any home—they have for centuries. The cooling effect of a fountain or waterfall on hot summer days and evenings will welcome visitors as they approach the front door. The esthetic effect of a fountain or pool will add untold appeal from the curb.

Planning, designing, and installing a water feature could be a lot of work—depending on its size—but there is nothing to say that you have to do it all yourself. There are many qualified landscape designers, landscape architects, and contractors who can help you along the way.

Working with a professional doesn't have to be an all-or-nothing proposition. For example, you can have a landscape architect or designer plan the feature and surrounding landscape for you, and then install it yourself. On the other hand, you can design the feature yourself and then hire a contractor to do the work. Ask friends and neighbors to recommend someone who has done work for them.

Although water gardens can be designed on a grandiose scale, there are smaller features—from sculpture fountains to tub gardens to birdbaths—that can add a splash of character to a particular part of the landscape. Both garden centers and home centers have a wide selection of water features from which to choose; mail-order houses are also a thriving part of this industry.

When budgeting for your water feature, you'll need to consider obvious expenses such as liner materials for pools and pumps for fountains, but don't forget to take into account the related costs. Landscaping elements, such as plants, flowers, and, perhaps, rocks and stones, may all be necessary to produce an attractive setting for the feature. If you choose to buy pond fish, such as koi, the cost of purchasing them and then caring for them will also add up.

The twin fountains spouting from this small-scale water garden add movement and sound to the landscape. The garden pool is surrounded by plants and flowers to give it a natural look.

LAWNS AND GROUND COVERS

There's a certain formality to a lawn that's pleasing to the eye. Its cool green expanse, with its uniform texture and color, will bestow a polished look on the front of any home.

Of the many hundreds of grasses that grow in the Northern Hemisphere, only about 40 types are usually cultivated as lawns. Many of those have numerous vari-eties developed to give you a multitude of choices. Grasses vary in their performance, appearance, watering needs, and maintenance requirements. Moreover, each grass has its own climate considerations. As a general rule, the way to keep a lawn looking healthy is to develop a maintenance schedule and stick to it. A lawn requires regular mowing, watering, and fertilizing.

This well-manicured lawn adds to the simple elegance of the home shown above. While it incorporates both trees and flowers into its layout, the lawn is still the focal point of the landscape. Any lawn can be kept healthy and green by following a set maintenance schedule.

Mowing: Grass types and seasons will dictate how often you should mow. During the active growing season, a lawn may need mowing every two or three days. However, off-season cutting may only be required every two weeks or once a month. As a simple rule of thumb, keep the grass short enough so that you never cut more than a third the length of each blade.

Watering: The best way to water your lawn is to soak the soil deeply and not water again until the top inch or two begins to dry out. Watering deeply allows grass roots to extend deeper into the soil. Deep roots are more resistant to drought. If you water too frequently, roots stay near the surface and don't penetrate deep enough to survive drought. Grass with deeper roots is also more resistant to disease.

Fertilizing: Experts don't always agree about the type and amount of fertilizer each lawn needs, but they do agree on one thing—most lawns require it. Lawns are unnatural environments where plants are crowded together. Therefore, they require higher amounts of nutrients than are available naturally; this is especially true of a lawn where the clippings, a natural fertilizer, are removed after mowing. Some fertilizers are mixed with herbicides for spring weed control. Choosing the right mixture and applying it correctly can save you time and money by allowing you to do two jobs in one. All fertilizers require a thorough watering after application. If left dry, most fertilizers will burn the lawn.

If your lawn needs more than just basic maintenance—if all or part of it needs to be replaced, for example—you'll have to replant using either seed or sod (below). Although the task of replacing a lawn is fairly labor intensive, it is still well within the ability of the average homeowner. You may, however, want to consult a landscaping professional for advice on specific issues, such as the type of grasses that grow well in your area. A professional can also advise you on how to deal with any grading or soil problems you may encounter.

Certain types of grasses survive in shady environments—cool-season fescues do well. You might want

A lush front lawn bisected by a crisp brick walkway functions like an outdoor living room for relaxation or recreation.

to consider planting a ground cover in areas that don't get much direct sunlight, as these plants are better suited to difficult growing conditions.

Ground covers range from woody shrubs to vines, and from spreading perennials to a few that are popularly thought of as bulbs. Within the rich assortment of ground covers you can find plants that will stand in for lawn; but you'll find a far greater number that will prosper in lawn-defeating situations, or where lawn maintenance is an ongoing headache.

Ground covers are the obvious solution for areas of deep shade, dry or poor soil, hot and dry expanses, steep slopes, and soil infiltrated by competing tree roots. Where water conservation is essential, certain ground covers are the only viable means of achieving an expanse of low verdure. As a bonus, many ground covers sprout colorful flowers.

SEED VS. SOD

Sod or seed? Each method has its pros and cons. Consider these: Seeded lawns take longer to install, and a lot of care to establish, but they are much less expensive than sod. With seed you can choose any suitable grass type for your lawn, or a custom blend or mixture to meet your needs. Also, seeded lawns often have deeper root systems, allowing for heavy use.

In some areas, seed is the only means to establish a lawn in a shaded area, as shade grasses often do not form good sod.

Sod is both easy to install and to establish. It must be well watered, but will not be ravaged by weeds, seedling diseases, washouts, or birds. It is also less messy. The bare earth associated with a seeded lawn can mean weeks of tracking dirt into your house while the lawn grows in.

Sod also simplifies growing a lawn around trees, as it will not compete with the tree's roots for nutrients the way sprouting seeds do. But sod is expensive, and doesn't offer a wide variety of grasses. And since it's grown on a layer of foreign soil, it may not bind well to its new soil.

TREES AND SHRUBS

Trees establish the landscape's general character in many ways: They provide shade, give a feeling of shelter, create perspective, and form a focal point. For one or all of these reasons, having trees planted in the front of your home will definitely add to its appeal.

Shrubs form the framework of a landscape—they're the stable plantings that influence views, direct circulation, and make a smooth transition from tree canopy to ground level. They can be used to punctuate the landscape in a less dominant manner than trees do; and, of course, they have a traditional use as a "foundation planting"—whether or not there's a house foundation to mask.

Using trees, shrubs, or the two in conjunction, you can not only create appealing views, but also form barriers to make the landscape at the front of your home more comfortable. Always consider the mature height of the tree or shrub you're choosing. You don't want to plant something that becomes too tall or unwieldy as it grows. Nursery professionals can help you when you make your selection; they can also provide tips on maintenance.

Of course, one of the most widely used landscape plantings is the hedge. Hedges can be used to define limits and ensure privacy—important considerations for any entry way. For tips on shaping a hedge, see the opposite page.

The shrubs and small trees at the front of this house add to the character of the facade without overpowering it. Bordering flowers add a touch of color to green backdrop.

SHAPING A HEDGE

A hedge is a living barrier or fence made up of many plants, usually of one species. When planted close enough together, and after several years of growth, the individual plants will appear to be one unit. Developing a hedge takes considerable planning and care in the first couple of seasons. After that, you can concentrate chiefly on routine maintenance.

There are two basic styles of hedges: Formal hedges are trimmed so that the sides are perfectly straight, creating a solid, smooth appearance. Informal hedges are pruned selectively, allowing the plants to achieve a more natural shape, with a look that is soft and feathery. The choice of hedge depends on the personal taste of the homeowner.

Space the plants 1 to 5 feet apart, depending on their current and intended sizes. After planting, cut the plants back considerably; smaller plants should be pruned to a height of 6 to 12 inches. This forces most species to branch out close to the ground, preventing an unsightly framework of bare, lower trunks. Don't trim plants during the first season, unless a strong stem grows higher than the rest. In that case, snip it back level with the rest of the hedge. Later, keep the hedge tapered, with the top narrower than the bottom *(bottom, left)*.

Tapering helps light reach the lower branches, keeping them healthy and leafy. Cutting back will create a dense and mature look. If your hedge has extra vigorous plants, you may need to prune it more than once a season.

1st Year

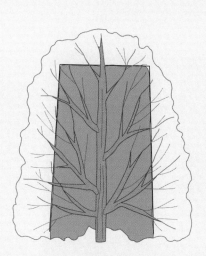

2nd Year

3rd Year

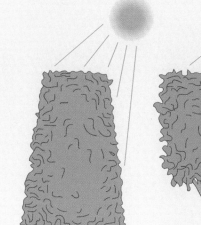

Right
Taper allows sunlight to reach entire plant.

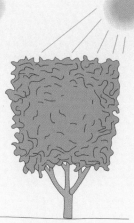

Wrong
Sunlight can't reach bottom of plant.

Formal

Informal

PLANTS AND FLOWERS

For most people, plants and flowers are the essence of the landscape—the living, constantly unfolding element of most immediate beauty. Their role as a beautifying element in the front of the home is obvious.

Homeowners have a wide selection of plants from which to choose. Local nurseries and, more and more, home centers have selections large enough to satisfy any taste. If you're having trouble choosing, the professionals at these stores can offer advice.

Every kind of plant has a distinctive texture, or visual surface, created by the size and shape of its leaves and the way it holds them to catch and reflect sunlight. Textures may be airy or dense, smooth or rough, fine or coarse. Two kinds of plants may have similar leaves but hold them so differently that their textures are quite dissimilar.

In designing your landscape, choose plants that have a variety of textures, but don't overdo it; maintain a continuity. Too many colors together can be confusing. Abrupt contrasts can be effective, but only if they are kept to a minimum. Otherwise it's best to graduate textures. You'll find that small areas seem larger if they're designed with fine-textured plants, whereas coarse textures can make large areas seem smaller.

To create an especially beautiful and functional environment, capitalize on the fact that some plants shed their leaves annually, while others keep them. Touches or masses of green lend life and substance to the winter landscape.

Plantings should combine harmonious colors representing a continuous segment of the color wheel: red, red violet, and violet, for example. The smaller the landscape, the narrower the segment should be.

A neutral zone of shrubs and ground cover around colorful flowers will make them even more noticeable, as will repeating color. Pots of blue pansies punctuate a smattering of the same color mixed in a bed of Antique Shades pansies.

Annuals, switched out two to three times a year, paint this front-yard landscape. In the fall (left), pansies and Sweet William fill the garden. Impatiens, caladiums, and torenia, shown below, take summer's heat and never miss a beat.

se complementary colors—those opposite one another on the color wheel—sparingly, for accents.

You can create striking contrasts by the occasional se of light and dark opposites—for example, light ellow marigolds with dark blue lobelia. To draw the ye to a focal point, dark or brilliant colors are appro-riate. Always use restraint—an attractive landscape is estful to the eye, rather than a source of constant stim-lation. A range of muted colors provides the most estful effect.

To brighten large areas, use the warm colors of the ed-orange-yellow range. Because they make a distant lanting seem closer, warm colors are also helpful at he rear of long, narrow areas.

The cool colors of the green-blue-violet range, on the ther hand, can make a shallow space appear deeper, nd will show to greater effect when massed.

Plant colors span a wide spectrum, and not only ithin the realm of flowers. In addition to dozens f shades of green, foliage can also be red, purple, lver, or gold.

Annuals and perennials are just as important in the ndscape picture as the usually permanent plantings f trees and shrubs. Most annuals and perennials are rown for the beauty of their flowers and the color npact these blossoms provide. In this respect they are ot different from many shrubs. But annuals last for just one flowering season, and the majority of perennials must be periodically divided and replanted—and therein lies their special landscape advantage; you can paint a new garden image easily by changing plants or by planting a different color of the same plant. Nurseries and mail-order plant suppliers carry a wide selection of annuals and perennials.

LIGHTING AND SECURITY

Visual appeal, safety, and security—all three are functions of successful entryway lighting, and all three can be achieved with the right fixtures and a well-designed lighting scheme.

With as few as two or three well placed outdoor lights, a front yard can take on the striking beauty of a garden at night, and at the same time become a safer place for family and friends alike. Lighting options are discussed starting on page 95.

While basic door and pathway lighting provides some security, adding lights to less obvious spots around the exterior of the house, or installing a separate security lighting system, improves security immeasurably. Security lighting is discussed on page 100.

Lights need power, and the type of power supply you require will depend on the lighting system you choose. Easily installed 12-volt systems are an energy efficient solution (*page 100*).

For ideas on security beyond lighting, read about central security systems on pages 102 and 103.

A warmly lit porch is a welcoming sight. Additional lawn fixtures highlight plantings, define space, and improve safety and security.

LIGHTING UP THE NIGHT

To be truly inviting, your entryway should be warmly lit. The lighting should also help direct guests through your front yard to your door.

Brighter lights work well to highlight the entrance to the driveway. If the route is long and wooded, softer lights can then be used very effectively to outline the rest of the way. Fixtures installed for this purpose should be low and soft enough to prevent glare in the drivers' eyes.

The garage area is often a good spot for security lighting, perhaps controlled by a sensor or timer (but always with an indoor switch for emergencies).

Front paths and steps are easiest to light if their surfaces are a light, reflective color. Low fixtures that spread soft pools of light can greet guests and highlight your garden's virtues along the walk. All steps along the path should be illuminated. Small fixtures next to the steps will do, or you may be able to build lights into the steps.

If your house has deep eaves or an overhang extending the length of your walk, you might consider installing weatherproof downlights to illuminate your walk and plantings without any visible fixtures.

At the front door, you'll want light for several purposes. In addition to lighting your house number and to welcoming guests, proper lighting will allow you to see a caller's face. If you choose decorative clear-glass fixtures, remember to keep low-wattage bulbs in them to avoid glare.

Illuminating foliage can be an effective way to combine functional and decorative lighting at the entryway. Uplighting, downlighting, and spread lighting are all common techniques (page 97). For a dappled, "moonlight" effect, place both uplights and downlights in a large tree. To silhouette a tree or shrub, aim a spotlight or wall-washer light at a fence or wall from close behind the plant. Decorative mini-lights help outline trees and lend sparkle to your garden.

You can create a number of interesting garden effects by placing uplights, downlights, and accent lights on separate switches. Dimmers, photocells, and timers can be used for even more flexibility and variety.

Outdoor fixtures

Outdoor lighting fixtures come in many variations, some depicted at right. Regardless of what you choose, you'll want to avoid glare. An opaque covering on a fixture will create a warm glow rather than a hot spot of light. You can also use lower light levels. At night, a little light goes a long way: 20 watts is considered "strong."

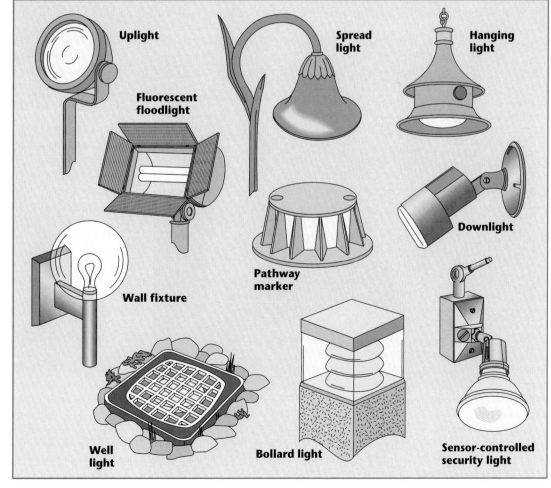

Uplight

Spread light

Hanging light

Fluorescent floodlight

Wall fixture

Pathway marker

Downlight

Well light

Bollard light

Sensor-controlled security light

These oversize carriage lanterns not only illuminate the way to the front door but, with their brick pillars, form a welcoming gateway for guests.

Effective downlighting illuminates tall trees along the front path. Additional fixtures near ground level add further lighting.

Outdoor lighting techniques

You can use the fixtures shown on page 95 to light up your surroundings in various imaginative ways. Some standard lighting techniques are illustrated here. You can also combine techniques for interesting results.

Downlighting
Use this technique to gently light up your porches, patios, and walkways. It's also good for accenting trees, shrubs and flowers, while letting you see where you're going at night.

Silhouetting
To silhouette a tree, shrub, or bed of flowers, try aiming a spotlight or wall washer at a fence or wall from close behind the plant.

Diffused lighting
A low level of lighting is often enough for low-traffic areas. Light railings and fences indirectly from underneath or behind to outline the edges of the structures.

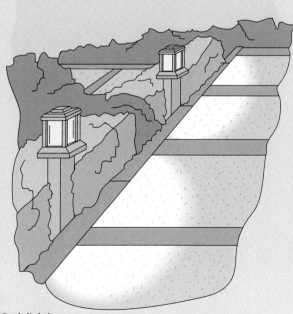

Path lighting
Low or slightly raised fixtures that spread soft pools of light can define a walkway and highlight elements of your garden.

Spread lighting
You can light up your shrubbery with spread lights in the planting beds themselves. Try different-colored bulbs for different effects.

A cobblestone pathway is lit from above by spotlights attached to the eaves. Stained-glass upstairs windows, lit from within, add a warm glow.
LIGHTING DESIGN: SUSAN HUEY, LUMINAE, INC.

SECURITY LIGHTING

The idea of security lighting sometimes conjures up images of blinding spotlights that keep a property brighter at night than it is during the day. However, this does not have to be the case.

SEPARATE LIGHTING SYSTEMS

Very good entryway security can be provided by an attractive garden lighting scheme that illuminates key spots beyond simply the path and doorway. By lighting—with standard garden fixtures—porch areas, house corners, low windows, as well as side and back doors, you can keep intruders from approaching your house without being observed. This kind of lighting should provide bright light where it's needed most and leave other areas less lighted for contrast.

As a backup to an integrated security lighting system, you can add a powerful 250-watt quartz floodlight for use in emergencies.

INTEGRATED SECURITY LIGHTING SYSTEMS

Separate security lighting systems can be a good addition to larger properties. On smaller properties, the addition of one or two extra security lights is an adequate precaution.

Lights designed specifically for security can be brighter than standard outdoor lights, but they do not necessarily have to dominate the landscape by being left on all night. Many types of switches and sensors are available for these systems. Wireless motion sensors, for example, use radio signals to activate your lights whenever someone enters your property. These systems can be set to turn off the lights again after a certain time has elapsed.

Another possibility is to control your security lights with a timer. This way the lights will turn on and off when you're away, just after you've gone to bed, or any other time you choose.

If you plan to keep your security lights on for extended periods, take precautions so you don't ruin the effect of the other lighting. For example, 30-watt high-pressure sodium lamps provide enough light for home security without being harsh and overly bright.

Sodium and mercury vapor lamps, and certain metal halide lamps have been specially designed for security use as well as energy efficiency. However, because these lamps take a few minutes to warm up, it's a good idea to incorporate one or two quartz incandescent lamps into your security lighting system to ensure bright light in an instant.

A well-lit front entry is crucial for good security. Here, a pair of handsome iron fixtures atop stone pillars bathe the doorway in light without creating glare. Low voltage spread lights define the garden borders and well lights accent the trees.

WIRING YOUR ENTRYWAY LIGHTS

Though you may not want to do the wiring for your entryway lighting, it's good to have a basic idea what is involved in the process. The entry lights at the doorway are probably on an inside circuit. Other outdoor lights will need their own system. The principles are the same for both indoor and outdoor wiring, but some materials used outdoors are specially designed to resist the weath. Raintight subpanel boxes and watertight switch boxes, fo example, remain safe in damp and wet locations.

Underground electrical cable has a thick solid plast covering that makes it watertight when buried direct in the ground. Typically, however, outdoor wiring is

ADDING A 12-VOLT SYSTEM

Some low-voltage lights come in a kit with a transformer. Be sure to use the proper size and type of wire (follow manufacturer's recommendations).

To install a low-voltage system for outdoor use, you'll need a transformer, usually housed in a water-resistant box, to step the household current of 120 volts down to 12 volts (24-volt systems are also available).

Mount the transformer near the weatherproof switch or receptacle and then run a cable a few inches below the ground from the low-voltage side of the transformer to the desired locations for your lights.

Some fixtures clip onto the wire; others must be wired into the system. If you don't already have an outlet, have an electrician install a GFCI-protected outlet *(below)*.

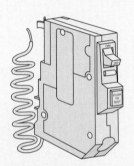

GFCI circuit or receptacle
According to present electrical codes, any new outside receptacle must be protected by a ground fault circuit interrupter (GFCI, or GFI). Whenever the amounts of incoming and outgoing current are not equal—indicating current leakage (a "ground fault")—the GFCI opens the circuit instantly, cutting off the power.

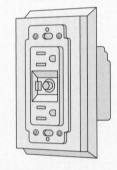

Circuit breaker GFCI

Receptacle GFCI

A typical 12-volt installation
Since a 12-volt system uses a greatly reduced voltage, special conduit and boxes of other outdoor wiring are not required. Most transformers are rated for home use from 25 to over 300 watts (volt amperes). The higher the rating, the more lengths of 100-foot cable—and consequently the more light fixtures—can be connected to the transformer. The total wattage of the lamps should not be less than half the transformer's volt ampere, or total nominal wattage (TNW) rating. Nor should it exceed the transformer's capacity. Most transformers are encased in raintight boxes; to be safe, though, plan to install yours at least a foot off the ground in a sheltered location.

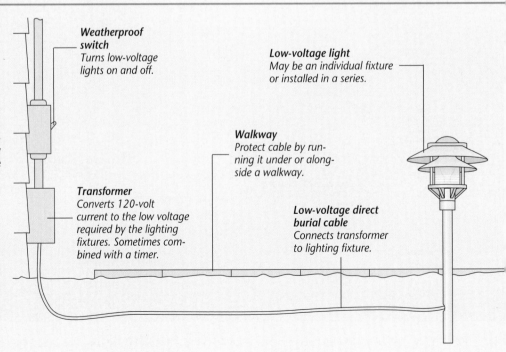

Weatherproof switch
Turns low-voltage lights on and off.

Low-voltage light
May be an individual fixture or installed in a series.

Walkway
Protect cable by running it under or alongside a walkway.

Transformer
Converts 120-volt current to the low voltage required by the lighting fixtures. Sometimes combined with a timer.

Low-voltage direct burial cable
Connects transformer to lighting fixture.

routed through rigid metallic and rigid nonmetallic conduits, which protect it from the weather and accidental damage. An electrician can create an outdoor outlet by tapping into an existing switch, lighting, or receptacle outlet box. A simpler alternative is low-voltage lighting. Operating on only 12 volts, low-voltage wiring is easy to install and doesn't present the dangers of 120 volts. Whatever the system, use the protection of ground fault circuit interrupters (GFCIs) on all outdoor circuits. You'll probably be able to install low-voltage lighting yourself, but for 120-volt lighting, it's usually best to consult an electrician.

ADDING A 120-VOLT SYSTEM

A 120-volt outdoor lighting system for your entryway offers several advantages. For starters, a light from a single fixture can illuminate a larger area—especially useful for security and for lighting trees from the ground. In addition, a 120-volt system offers flexibility: not only light fixtures, but also power tools, patio heaters, and electric garden tools can be plugged into 120-volt outdoor outlets.

A 120-volt outdoor system consists of a set of fixtures, of course, and some underground type UF 120-volt cable or conduit; the length used depends on the locations of the fixtures and wires. Your electrician will probably connect the system through an indoor switch and timer to an existing electrical source or circuit, as shown below. This will allow you to turn lights on and off by hand or let the timer do it for you.

The diagrams shown here will help you understand the basics of a 120-volt system. But unless you are skilled at this kind of work, you should leave the job to a professional.

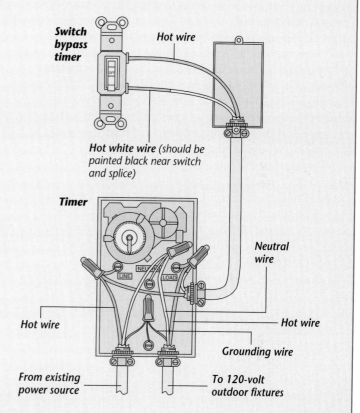

Switch bypass timer
Hot wire
Hot white wire (should be painted black near switch and splice)
Timer
Neutral wire
Hot wire
Hot wire
Grounding wire
From existing power source
To 120-volt outdoor fixtures

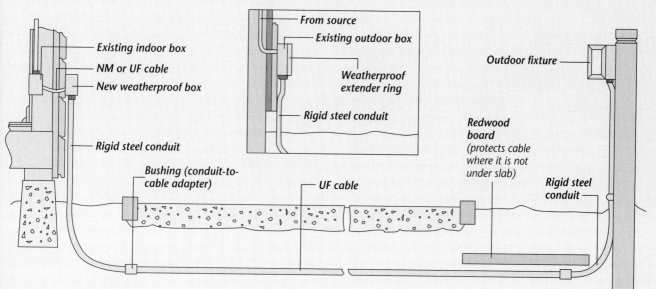

Existing indoor box
NM or UF cable
New weatherproof box
Rigid steel conduit
Bushing (conduit-to-cable adapter)
From source
Existing outdoor box
Weatherproof extender ring
Rigid steel conduit
UF cable
Outdoor fixture
Redwood board (protects cable where it is not under slab)
Rigid steel conduit

120-volt wiring at a glance
The illustration above depicts a standard outdoor wiring setup, using a 120-volt system. The outdoor fixture, housed in the weatherproof box, is attached by a rigid steel conduit to the existing indoor circuit structure. The outdoor outlet must be GFCI protected. You must place the cable 2 or more feet underground. To wire an indoor switch and timer for 120-volt outdoor fixtures, see the illustration above, top.

SECURITY SYSTEMS

W hile the right lighting can show off your property to great effect at night—and improve security at the same time—the components of a security system are generally hidden away, adding nothing to the attractiveness of your house—but adding greatly to your safety and peace of mind.

In recent years, concern over crime, along with the encouragement of law enforcement agencies and insurance companies, have turned security systems into one of the fastest-selling accessories for the home. And, no wonder. The FBI Uniform Crime Report shows a staggering number of burglaries a year in the U.S. Having a home security system can help ensure that you avoid being one of these statistics.

SYSTEMS AND SENSORS
The most effective home security system is a central system, in which a network of interconnected sensors and alarms can be controlled from a central control box or module (in a wireless system, this can be a hand-held touch pad).

There are two general types of central home security systems: wireless and hard-wired (although some systems are a combination of the two). In a wireless system, battery-powered sensors communicate with the control box by radio signal; in a hard-wired system, each sensor is connected to a main control box with wires.

With no wires stretching from sensors to control box, wireless systems are much easier to install (requiring just an hour or two and very few tools), though they can be more expensive.

PERIMETER PROTECTION
For full protection, it's vital to have a contact sensor at every point of entry easily accessible to an intruder. Door and window sensors protect your home by detecting unwanted intrusions and sending a signal to the control box. To alert the system when a window is broken, additional glass-breaking detectors can be installed to set off the alarm at the sound of shattering glass. Typically, when a sensor has detected an intrusion, an alarm or alarms are activated; lights and other appliances can also be controlled and triggered by the security system. In addition, the control boxes of most security systems have an automatic dialer that can be programmed to call a local security company or any other relevant number.

As well as a sensor at every entry point, interior sensors are included in many security systems, in the event that an intruder manages to make it into the house. These sensors function by detecting heat, movement, or the interruption of a light beam or a field of low energy radiation.

Incandescent floodlight
Controlled by a switch inside the house and activated by a motion sensor.

POINTS OF SECURITY
The house illustrated above is protected by a security lighting system and a central home security system. The lights provide a perimeter of illumination that acts as a first line of defense against intruders. The

Alarm (hidden under eaves)
Sirens, bells, horns, or other alarms are triggered by the control panel when an intrusion has been detected, or in case of fire if the system includes smoke detectors. It is best to have at least one alarm inside the house as well.

Door/window sensors
Sensors on doors and windows provide protection for your home and family by detecting unwanted intrusion through a door or window and reporting the situation to the control box.

Mercury-vapor post lamp
Controlled by a switch in the house and left on all night.

Glass-break sensor
A glass-break sensor detects the sudden shock of glass breaking and reports it to the control box, setting off the alarm.

specific requirements for a security lighting system vary from house to house, but the basic principles shown above can be applied in many situations. As illustrated, the central security system provides sensors at each potential point of entry.

DESIGN: PETER WHITELEY

DEFINING YOUR BORDERS

Like placing a beautiful painting in a frame, enclosing a property within a wall, hedge, or fence creates a look of completeness. The traditional charm of a white picket fence, the formal symmetry of a brick wall, the pastoral appeal of a flowering hedge—any one of these additions can succeed in tying together all the landscaping and architectural features it surrounds.

Depending on your needs, a wall, hedge, or fence can serve many other functions as well, from improving safety and security to increasing privacy. When considering your options, always balance esthetic concerns with functional requirements (and check local building and zoning codes). A tall fence will create privacy, for example, but it may also seem imposing from the street. A solution might be to install a shorter fence and plant taller shrubs in strategic places to block out unwanted views. Leaf through the following pages for more ideas.

Painted the same color as the trim on the house, this picket fence creates a homespun sense of unity and order. Picket fences work particularly well with Victorian, Colonial, Cape Cod, and ranch-style houses.

SHRUBS AND HEDGES

ust a few shrubs can effectively outline the edge of a
front lawn, or any other garden area. Some shrubs
row quickly and can be set in place for immediate
ffect. Others take longer to fill out. Their decorative
ses are varied; they can introduce a burst of floral col-
r and a wide spectrum of textures and shades of green.
y planting a number of shrubs of the same species
lose together in a row, you'll produce a hedge. A hedge
an be allowed to grow high and thick, providing an
mple screen against neighbors or traffic on the street.
Or, with careful trimming the hedge becomes a formal
landscaping element, providing a degree of privacy
but leaving at least part of the property open to view.
Hedges can also provide a good backdrop for perennials
or annuals. In any event, the best plants to use are those
that produce dense foliage from the ground up.

Compared to other features that delineate space—like
fences or walls—hedges and shrubs require more in the
way of ongoing care. For example, pruning shrubs of
damaged or diseased wood should be done several times
a year. As winter approaches, some shrubs may need to
be physically shielded from the elements.

*ose bushes grow high and wild, filling the front garden with flowers while revealing an intriguing glimpse of the lovely old farm-
ouse beyond. In a formal setting, carefully tended hedges can be trimmed to a desired shape and height.*

WALLS

A wall can be an elegant boundary marker that will serve its purpose for generations. Indeed, many of the oldest surviving structures on the planet are stone walls. In planning for a wall, carefully consider how the wall style will fit within the entryway. A carefully mortared brick wall, for example, suits a formal setting, while a wall made of uncut stone often has a more rustic appeal. The wall should also complement or echo the architecture of the house. You can either make the wall of the same material as the house—brick, stone, and even clapboard or stucco

are all possibilities—or choose a detail from the hou and use it on the wall.

Keep in mind that while the results can be particular distinctive, building a wall is a more daunting underta ing than putting up a fence or planting a hedge. Als the materials used in wall construction—often ston and brick—can be very expensive, and because of th great weight, cost that much more to have delivered Many garden walls must be built over a concrete foo ing or foundation, although some dry stone walls on need a gravel base.

A stone retaining wall creates the feeling of an entry courtyard, which functions like a garden foyer for receiving visitors.

A wall of rough-edged bricks supports colorful hanging plants, creating a solid barrier that looks right at home in a lush garden environment.

ombining privacy and elegance, container plants
nd columns of recycled bricks (above) accent a tall
ooden gate at the opening to an entry courtyard.

A section of brick wall (right) helps define the
boundary of a small front patio while coordinating
nicely with the entryway's brick pathway. The wall
provides a backdrop for an array of plants and leads
the eye toward the bright blue concrete steps.

FENCES

With fences available in a near-endless variety of styles and materials, there is bound to be a front fence design that will complement the look of your home and garden.

Low or open fences can physically separate areas—providing a sense of security—while visually preserving a feeling of openness and welcome. For example, a traditional picket fence serves as a barrier, but does so in an unimposing way, and still succeeds in setting off the front yard with charm and grace.

To further balance a sense of welcome with the enclosure provided by a fence, pay particular attention to the gates or other openings along the fence. Introducing an interesting gate design and setting it off with flowering plants will draw the eye and lead visitors through the fence and up the front path.

Plants can also be put to good esthetic use along the length of the fence. For example, fences can be designed to support vines or to act as a backdrop for planting be The color and texture of a fence can complement the c or and texture of plantings placed next to it. An examp is the traditional combination of red roses backed a white picket fence.

Another good way to introduce a splash of vibra color to the edge of a fence is to plant annuals. Mar bloom about three weeks after the last frost and wi remain colorful all summer long. Fences can als serve as a support or backdrop for planting stru tures like trellises, raised planter boxes, and hangi planters. For ideas on using fences as a backdrop f plants, turn to the illustrations on page 110-11 For more on plants, see page 92.

A vine-covered arbor (above) creates a welcoming gateway through a picket fence. Colorful plantings contrast effectively with the bright white of the pickets and house trim.

An elegant wrought-iron fence (right) acts as a solid barrier between the street and the yard without blocking off views or appearing imposing.

A rustic post and rail fence and accompanying bank of flowers create a border in keeping with the rural location and special appeal of the stone house at left.

PLANTS AND THE FENCE

Plants add immeasurably to the attractiveness of any fence, wall, or screen and thus enhance the look of the entryway as a whole.

For plants to thrive against a fence, they must receive the right amount of sun and shade for their species. But plants that normally need full sun may literally bake when grown against fences facing west or south, especially those painted white or another light color.

One way of avoiding such a heat trap is to allow for air circulation around the plants: Either position them several feet away from the fence or arrange for air circulation through the fence itself by removing a few fence boards near the shrubs. Or use a different fence design.

If the fence runs east to west, the north side will b[e] shady; choose shade-loving plants for that side. Th[e] east side of a fence running north to south will be cool[er] than the west side; it can provide an ideal place for plan[ts] that thrive in partial sunlight.

A fence can provide a backdrop for plants; it can pr[o]vide needed support for vines and espaliers (below), an[d] it can support potted plants, either on shelves or han[g]ing from brackets.

A fence can also be camouflaged by plants, so if yo[u] prefer not to see your fence, use plants to hide it. Plan[ts] can completely obscure a fence or soften its lines so th[at] it blends with the landscape.

Your fence can be a backdrop
Decorative shrubs and other plants often appear at their best when displayed against a fence or screen; bold leaves and interesting shapes don't get lost in the surrounding vegetation.

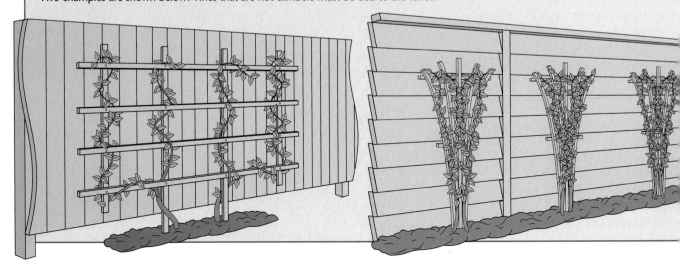

Vines can climb a fence
Climbing vines quickly adorn new fences and screens with foliage. Though a few will cling to a solid fence (notably Boston and English ivies), most vines require openwork on which to climb. Two examples are shown below. Vines that are not climbers must be tied to the fence.

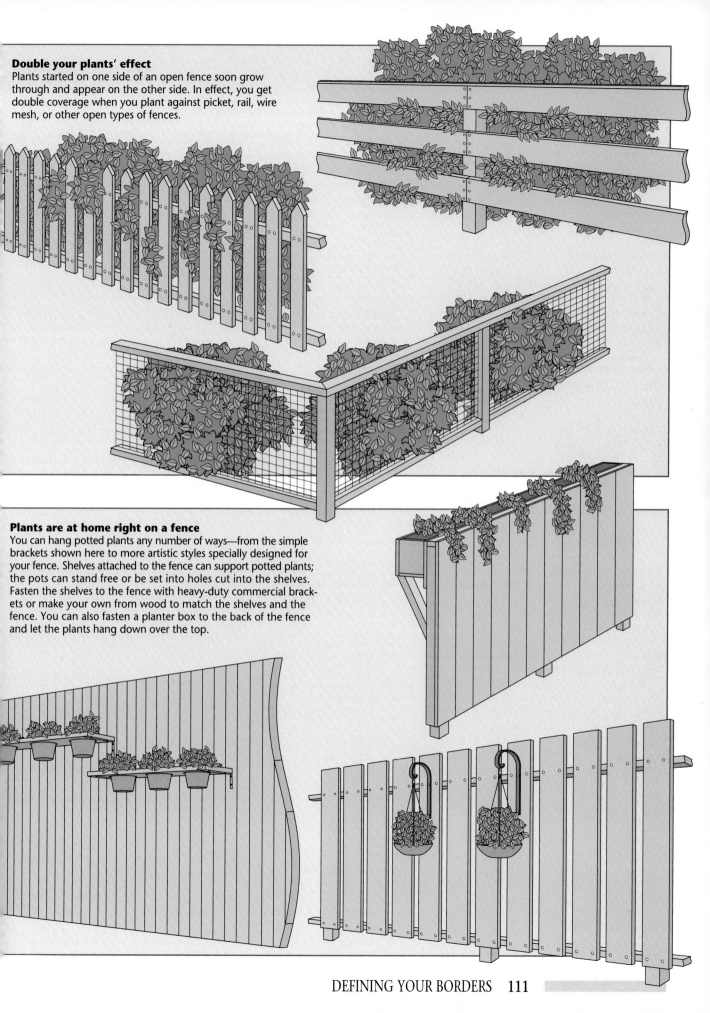

Double your plants' effect
Plants started on one side of an open fence soon grow through and appear on the other side. In effect, you get double coverage when you plant against picket, rail, wire mesh, or other open types of fences.

Plants are at home right on a fence
You can hang potted plants any number of ways—from the simple brackets shown here to more artistic styles specially designed for your fence. Shelves attached to the fence can support potted plants; the pots can stand free or be set into holes cut into the shelves. Fasten the shelves to the fence with heavy-duty commercial brackets or make your own from wood to match the shelves and the fence. You can also fasten a planter box to the back of the fence and let the plants hang down over the top.

INDEX